Given to

the library

in memory of

OSCAR MARING

THE FIGHT FOR CHATTANOOGA

Chickamauga to Missionary Ridge

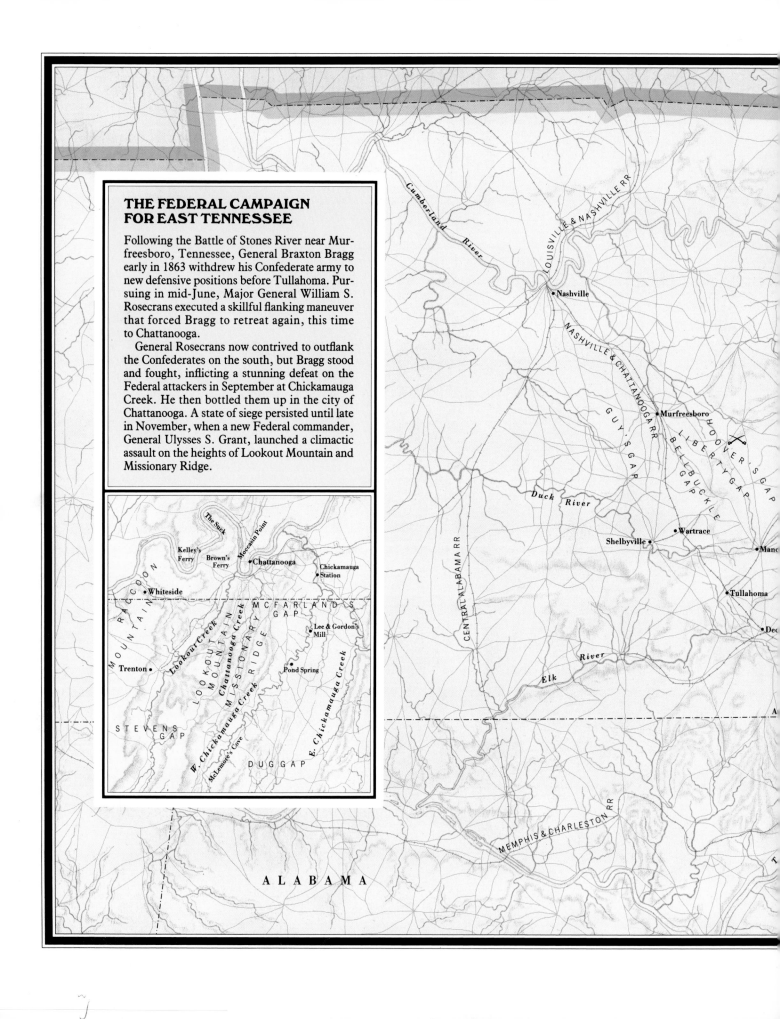

THE FEDERAL CAMPAIGN FOR EAST TENNESSEE

Following the Battle of Stones River near Murfreesboro, Tennessee, General Braxton Bragg early in 1863 withdrew his Confederate army to new defensive positions before Tullahoma. Pursuing in mid-June, Major General William S. Rosecrans executed a skillful flanking maneuver that forced Bragg to retreat again, this time to Chattanooga.

General Rosecrans now contrived to outflank the Confederates on the south, but Bragg stood and fought, inflicting a stunning defeat on the Federal attackers in September at Chickamauga Creek. He then bottled them up in the city of Chattanooga. A state of siege persisted until late in November, when a new Federal commander, General Ulysses S. Grant, launched a climactic assault on the heights of Lookout Mountain and Missionary Ridge.

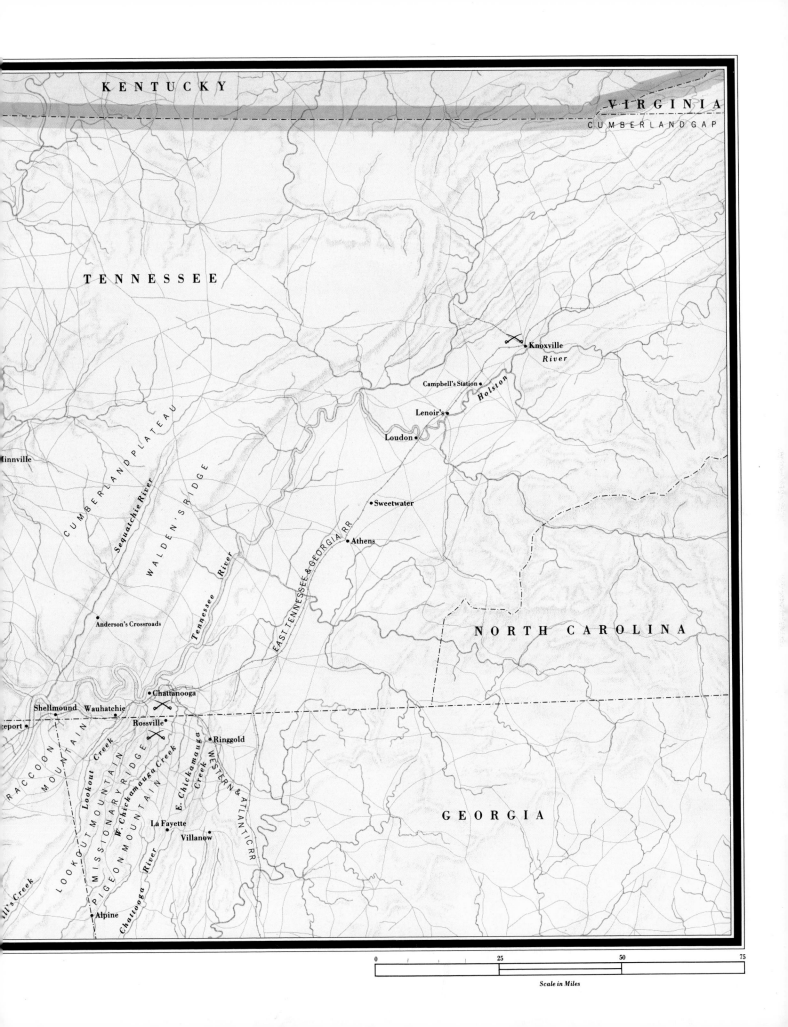

KENTUCKY

VIRGINIA

CUMBERLAND GAP

TENNESSEE

Knoxville
River

Campbell's Station •
Holston

Lenoir's •

Loudon •

Minnville •

Sweetwater •

CUMBERLAND PLATEAU

Sequatchie River

WALDEN'S RIDGE

Athens •

EAST TENNESSEE & GEORGIA R.R.

NORTH CAROLINA

Anderson's Crossroads •

Tennessee River

Chattanooga

Shellmound • Wauhatchie

eport •

Rossville •

Ringgold •

RACCOON MOUNTAIN

Lookout Creek

LOOKOUT MOUNTAIN

MISSIONARY RIDGE

W. Chickamauga Creek

PIGEON MOUNTAIN

E. Chickamauga Creek

Chattooga River

WESTERN & ATLANTIC R.R.

GEORGIA

La Fayette •

Villanow •

ll's Creek

Alpine •

0   25   50   75

Scale in Miles

TIME
LIFE
BOOKS

Other Publications:

MYSTERIES OF THE UNKNOWN
TIME FRAME
FIX IT YOURSELF
FITNESS, HEALTH & NUTRITION
SUCCESSFUL PARENTING
HEALTHY HOME COOKING
UNDERSTANDING COMPUTERS
LIBRARY OF NATIONS
THE ENCHANTED WORLD
THE KODAK LIBRARY OF CREATIVE PHOTOGRAPHY
GREAT MEALS IN MINUTES
PLANET EARTH
COLLECTOR'S LIBRARY OF THE CIVIL WAR
THE EPIC OF FLIGHT
THE GOOD COOK
WORLD WAR II
HOME REPAIR AND IMPROVEMENT
THE OLD WEST

For information on and a full description of any of the
Time-Life Books series listed above, please write:
Reader Information
Time-Life Customer Service
P.O. Box C-32068
Richmond, Virginia 23261-2068
Or call: 1-800-621-7026

This volume is one of a series that chronicles in full the
events of the American Civil War, 1861-1865.
Other books in the series include:

The Cover: Urged on by their hat-waving
commander, Lieutenant Colonel Judson W. Bishop,
infantrymen of the 2nd Minnesota reach the
crest of Missionary Ridge on November 25, 1863,
in a triumphant assault on the seemingly
impregnable Confederate position.

THE
CIVIL
WAR

THE FIGHT FOR CHATTANOOGA

BY

JERRY KORN

AND THE

EDITORS OF TIME-LIFE BOOKS

Chickamauga to Missionary Ridge

TIME-LIFE BOOKS, ALEXANDRIA, VIRGINIA

The Civil War
Series Director: Henry Woodhead
Designer: Edward Frank
Series Administrator: Philip Brandt George

Editorial Staff for *The Fight for Chattanooga*
Associate Editor: Jane Coughran (pictures)
Staff Writers: Thomas H. Flaherty Jr., R. W. Murphy,
Daniel Stashower, David S. Thomson
Researchers: Stephanie Lewis, Brian C. Pohanka
(principals); Harris J. Andrews, Patti H. Cass
Assistant Designer: Cynthia T. Richardson
Copy Coordinator: Jayne E. Rohrich
Picture Coordinator: Betty H. Weatherley
Editorial Assistant: Donna Fountain
Special Contributors: Thomas A. Lewis, Brian McGinn,
Mark Moss

Editorial Operations
Design: Ellen Robling (assistant director)
Copy Chief: Diane Ullius
Editorial Operations: Caroline A. Boubin (manager)
Production: Celia Beattie
Quality Control: James J. Cox (director), Sally Collins
Library: Louise D. Forstall

Correspondents: Elisabeth Kraemer-Singh (Bonn);
Margot Hapgood, Dorothy Bacon (London); Miriam
Hsia (New York); Maria Vincenza Aloisi, Josephine du
Brusle (Paris); Ann Natanson (Rome). Valuable
assistance was also provided by: F. Lynne Bachleda
(Nashville) and Carolyn Chubet (New York).

The Author:
Jerry Korn won the Distinguished Flying Cross as a B-24
copilot in World War II; he then worked as a reporter for
the Associated Press before becoming an editor for *Collier's* and *Life*. He served for 12 years as the managing
editor of Time-Life Books. He is also the author of *The
Raising of the Queen*, the story of a maritime salvage operation, and of *War on the Mississippi* in the Time-Life Books
Civil War series.

The Consultants:
Colonel John R. Elting, USA (Ret.), a former Associate
Professor at West Point, is the author of *Battles for Scandi-
navia* in the Time-Life Books World War II series and of
*The Battle of Bunker's Hill, The Battles of Saratoga, Mili-
tary History and Atlas of the Napoleonic Wars, American
Army Life* and *The Superstategists*. Co-author of *A
Dictionary of Soldier Talk*, he is also editor of the three
volumes of *Military Uniforms in America, 1755-1867*, and
associate editor of *The West Point Atlas of American Wars*.

William A. Frassanito, a Civil War historian and lecturer
specializing in photograph analysis, is the author of two
award-winning studies, *Gettysburg: A Journey in Time* and
*Antietam: The Photographic Legacy of America's Bloodiest
Day*, and a companion volume, *Grant and Lee, The Virginia Campaigns*. He has also served as chief consultant to the
photographic history series *The Image of War*.

Les Jensen, Director of the Second Armored Division
Museum, Fort Hood, Texas, specializes in Civil War arti-
facts and is a conservator of historic flags. He is a contribu-
tor to *The Image of War* series, consultant for numerous
Civil War publications and museums, and a member of
the Company of Military Historians. He was formerly Curator of the U.S. Army Transportation Museum at Fort
Eustis, Virginia, and before that Curator of the Museum
of the Confederacy in Richmond, Virginia.

Michael McAfee specializes in military uniforms and has
been Curator of Uniforms and History at the West Point
Museum since 1970. A fellow of the Company of Military
Historians, he coedited with Colonel Elting *Long Endure:
The Civil War Years*, and he collaborated with Frederick
Todd on *American Military Equipage*. He is the author of
Artillery of the American Revolution, 1775-1783, and has
written numerous articles for *Military Images Magazine*.

James P. Shenton, Professor of History at Columbia University, is a specialist in 19th Century American political
and social history, with particular emphasis on the Civil
War period. He is the author of *Robert John Walker* and
Reconstruction South.

Library of Congress Cataloguing in Publication Data
Korn, Jerry.
  The fight for Chattanooga.
  (The Civil War)
  Bibliography: p.
  Includes index.
  1. Tennessee — History — Civil War, 1861-1865 —
Campaigns. 2. Chicamauga, Battle of, 1863.
3. Chattanooga, Battle of, 1863. 4. Lookout Mountain,
Battle of, 1863. 5. Missionary Ridge, Battle of, 1863.
I. Time-Life Books.   II. Title.   III. Series.
E470.5.K74 1985   973.7'359   85-13981
ISBN 0-8094-4816-5
ISBN 0-8094-4817-3 (lib. bdg.)

CONTENTS

Making War in Rough Country

The soldiers of General William Rosecrans' Federal army were awed by the natural beauty of the countryside as they advanced toward the strategic city of Chattanooga in September 1863. "Far beyond mortal vision extended one vast panorama of mountains, forests and rivers," one veteran recalled. "This is a beautiful valley," another wrote home, "with mountain tops on every side reaching up into the clouds."

The great hills were the Cumberlands, a southwestern spur of the Appalachians extending through Tennessee into northern Georgia. Yet for all its majesty, this isolated countryside was a hellish place to fight — the most formidable terrain in which major Federal and Confederate forces would clash during the entire Civil War.

The approaching Federals were hampered by burned-out bridges and a scarcity of roads. The shimmering, winding Tennessee River was shallow and turbulent — ill suited for supply vessels and yet a hindrance to maneuvering troops.

The knife-edge ridges prevented Rosecrans from seeing the army of his adversary, General Braxton Bragg, and equally masked the Federal host from Bragg's view. Most of the forested valleys and coves were narrow and cramped, natural traps that made ambush a constant threat. A sanguine Confederate predicted that Rosecrans "would dash himself to pieces against the many and vast natural barriers that rise all around Chattanooga."

When Rosecrans finally closed with Bragg in this magnificent but forbidding terrain, the ensuing battles made famous the scenes shown on these pages.

The view north from Lookout Mountain, one of the Cumberlands' highest ramparts at 2,126 feet, includes the horseshoe bend made by the Tennessee River as it meanders just west of Chattanooga. The mountain, said a Confederate, was all "gorges, boulders and jutting cliffs."

Lula Lake, part of a watercourse on a flank of Lookout Mountain, changed hands several times during the battles around Chattanooga. The wilderness pool was the

...primary source of drinking water on the mountain. The weary, dusty troops also used it to bathe, wash their clothes and water their horses.

The densely wooded valley cut by West Chickamauga Creek in the vicinity of Lee and Gordon's Mill, approximately 12 miles south of Chattanooga, was the

ene of one of the confused skirmishes that started the two-day Battle of Chickamauga.

The western slope of Missionary Ridge (*foreground*) dominates Chattanooga and the Tennessee River. This huge ridge, held through the late autumn of 1863 by stro▸

Confederate forces, looked to a Northern newspaperman like "an everlasting thunderstorm that will never pass over."

Aided by a windlass onshore, a steamboat on the Tennessee emerges from a turbulent narrows called The Suck. At various times boats on the Tennessee helped suppl

oth contending armies in the rugged Cumberlands with food and ammunition.

Breakthrough at Tullahoma

"I believe the most fatal errors of this war have begun in an impatient desire of success, that would not take time to get ready; the next fatal mistake being to be afraid to move when all the means were provided."

MAJOR GENERAL WILLIAM S. ROSECRANS, USA

During the first six months of 1863, the armies of Confederate General Braxton Bragg and Union Major General William S. Rosecrans lay no more than 30 miles apart in central Tennessee, menacing each other's supply lines with cavalry raids but otherwise inactive. Rosecrans, victor in the bloody Battle of Stones River at the turn of the year, had set up camp around the town of Murfreesboro, scene of the fighting. Bragg, after withdrawing to the southeast, had dug in along the Duck River, with his headquarters in the little railroad town of Tullahoma.

The Federal victory at Stones River had been costly and inconclusive. It had boosted morale in the Union after the Federal setbacks in 1862. But Bragg's Army of Tennessee still blocked Rosecrans and his Army of the Cumberland from their prime objective — Chattanooga, 80 miles away. This insignificant-looking settlement of 3,500 people on the Tennessee River occupied one of the most important strategic locations of the War — the intersection of several of the South's most important rail lines.

The armies lay athwart the main line of the Nashville & Chattanooga Railroad and transported their supplies on it — Rosecrans from the north, Bragg from the south. Just southwest of Chattanooga, at Stevenson, that line met the Memphis & Charleston Railroad from Vicksburg and the west; just east of the city, the Western & Atlantic Railroad came up from Atlanta and then snaked northeastward toward Richmond as the East Tennes-

see & Georgia. Over these rail routes flowed a great percentage of the Confederacy's arms, munitions, textiles, foodstuffs and manufactures. "If we can hold Chattanooga and Eastern Tennessee," Abraham Lincoln would later write, "I think the rebellion must dwindle and die."

And so it was clear that Rosecrans would have to try again to drive through Bragg to Chattanooga. His superiors in Washington urged him to move fast, before the Confederates could reinforce Bragg — or, conversely, before some of Bragg's troops might be detached to tip the balance against Federal forces elsewhere.

Indeed there was another prize at stake equally as important as Chattanooga — the Mississippi River port of Vicksburg. Major General Ulysses S. Grant was preparing to attack Vicksburg, 400 miles west of Murfreesboro. Grant's forces outnumbered the Confederate defenders under Lieutenant General John C. Pemberton. But the authorities in Washington were justifiably concerned that General Joseph E. Johnston, the overall Confederate commander in the West, might gamble on Rosecrans' inactivity and send reinforcements from Bragg to Pemberton. This would tip the odds against Grant. "I would not push you to any rashness," Lincoln wrote to Rosecrans, "but I am very anxious that you do your utmost, short of rashness, to keep Bragg from getting off to help Johnston against Grant."

But Rosecrans was not to be hurried. The

The model of a gallant leader, Major General William Starke Rosecrans gallops through shot and shell on a song-sheet cover that was published in his native Ohio at the height of his fame in 1863. Rosecrans impressed his staff and troops with his courage and strategic cunning. "With Rosecrans to lead," wrote one of his junior officers, "we think we can go anywhere in the Confederacy."

burly general had performed creditably early in the War. His aggressive use of smaller commands, his personal courage in battle and his concern for his men had won him the admiration of the public and his army. But he had driven his superiors in Washington to distraction with his lengthy preparations for any move; and now, after his victory at Stones River, he was doing it again.

Rosecrans argued that his men were tired; the army was low on rations. He needed time to strengthen his lines of communication and replenish his supplies. And although his force was considerably larger than Bragg's army, he felt that in order to wage an offensive campaign he needed to have even more troops, both infantry and cavalry.

As for Vicksburg, Rosecrans had evolved a novel military concept: If Bragg were driven out of Tennessee, he might abandon the area entirely and join Pemberton against Grant. Thus Rosecrans reasoned that he was protecting Grant by not attacking Bragg. As a clincher to his argument, Rosecrans cited what he said was a military axiom: No nation should fight two decisive battles at once. No one else seemed to have heard of this axiom — and General Grant, for one, was thoroughly exasperated by it. "It would be bad to be defeated in two decisive battles fought the same day," he later pointed out, "but it would not be bad to win them."

Yet Rosecrans stayed where he was and continued his lengthy preparations. Major General Thomas L. Crittenden, who commanded Rosecrans' XXI Corps, complained that after defeating the Confederates at Stones River the Federals "virtually went into hospital for six months before we could march after them again." The men built log huts around Murfreesboro and even planted rows of cedars along the company streets. As the weather warmed, there was plenty of drill. But for the most part, boredom reigned. Lieutenant William B. Rippetoe of the 18th Indiana Light Artillery said that when he was not reading or writing letters he spent his time "talking, eating, sleeping and fighting flies." Another Federal lamented that the men were "simply rusting away."

Thirty miles distant, the hungry Confederates foraged, hunted rabbits, practiced the manual of arms and waited. "It is a bad thing for an army to remain too long at one place," Private Sam Watkins of the 1st Tennessee wrote later. "The men soon became discontented and unhappy, and we had no diversion or pastime except playing poker or chuck-a-luck."

Only the cavalry was spared the general ennui. In January, Bragg had said that although his army was too short of manpower and rations to attack, he would fight if Rosecrans advanced and would "harass him if he does not." His chief engine of harassment was his large force of superb horsemen, led by some of the great cavalry commanders of the War: the diminutive Fighting Joe Wheeler, then only 27 years old, Nathan Bedford Forrest, John Hunt Morgan and — until he was slain on May 8 by a jealous husband — Earl Van Dorn. All told, Bragg had 15,000 horsemen in his army of 47,000, and during the early months of 1863 they badgered the Federals mercilessly.

A particular and frequent target of the Confederate cavalry raids was the Louisville & Nashville Railroad, over which Rosecrans received the bulk of his supplies. The superintendent of the railroad reported in July 1863 that the line had been fully operational for only seven of the previous 12 months. "All the bridges and trestleworks on the main stem and branches, with the exception of the bridge over Barren River and four small bridges, were destroyed and rebuilt during the year. Some of the structures were destroyed twice and some three times. In addition to this, most of the water stations, several depots and a large number of cars were burnt, a number of engines badly damaged, and a tunnel in Tennessee nearly filled up for a distance of eight hundred feet."

Rosecrans attempted to retaliate, but with little success. "Expeditions go out occasion-

ally to different parts of the country," Brigadier General John Beatty observed in February, "and slight affairs occur, which are magnified into serious engagements." He offered as an example a recent encounter in which the colonel of the 123rd Illinois claimed to have killed many Confederates and to have captured 300 rifles. "The truth," said Beatty, "is that he did not take time to count the rebel dead, and the arms taken were one hundred old muskets found in a house by the roadside."

Rosecrans, who had about 9,000 troopers, pestered Washington for more cavalry. He got none, but he did receive permission to make some of his foot soldiers mounted infantrymen. Thus was born one of the most colorful — and effective — brigades of the western war. The troops selected for mounted duty were the 1,500 men of the 17th and 72nd Indiana regiments and the 98th and 123rd Illinois; their commander was a tall Indiana colonel, John T. Wilder, who had owned an iron foundry in civilian life.

Making troopers of Wilder's foot soldiers was not easy. The men had to scrounge their own mounts from the countryside. An initial sweep yielded 300 horses and mules, but the men kept looking until they were all mounted on horses. Since they would fight dismounted, there was the matter of a suitable weapon for hand-to-hand combat; Wilder issued long-handled hatchets. That drew a derisive nickname — the Hatchet Brigade — but Wilder more than made up for it with his choice of firearms. After witnessing a demonstration by the gun's inventor, Christopher Spencer, Wilder ordered the seven-shot Spencer repeating rifles directly from the factory, paying for the guns by taking out a personal loan. Each man agreed to pay

Wilder for his rifle through payroll deductions; but before the troopers began payment, the embarrassed government stepped in to buy the weapons.

By June, Rosecrans had as many horsemen as did Bragg — whose cavalry had been reduced by transfers and losses to around 10,000. Moreover, infantry reinforcements had been sent to Rosecrans from Kentucky, and his army outnumbered Bragg's by a substantial margin — 70,000 to 40,000. His supply lines were now well protected, and he had been able to gather and store food and forage aplenty. By June the weather was good for marching.

Still Rosecrans did not move. The messages from Washington took on a biting tone. "I deem it my duty," General in Chief Henry W. Halleck wired Rosecrans on June 11, "to repeat to you the great dissatisfaction felt here at your inactivity."

Grant was besieging Vicksburg; the town's surrender was merely a matter of time, and Rosecrans had lost his last reason for delaying. On June 16, Halleck sent Rosecrans a curt and demanding message: "Is it your intention to make an immediate move forward? A definite answer, yes or no, is required." Rosecrans' reply was airy — almost insubordinate — but it also held a promise. "If 'immediate' means tonight or tomorrow," he said, "no. If it means as soon as all things are ready, say five days, yes."

Five days later, on June 21, the Army of the Cumberland was still in Murfreesboro. Halleck was doubtless furious, but he cannot have been surprised. Then on June 24 a wire arrived in Washington: "The army begins to move at 3 o'clock this morning." Suddenly Rosecrans' hesitation and uncertainty ended, and this man of many excuses

A Federal foraging party plunders livestock from a Tennessee farm despite angry protests from the farmfolk in one of a series of paintings by newspaper artist William D. T. Travis. The artist accompanied General Rosecrans' army for more than a year between 1862 and 1863.

began to act with boldness and confidence.

Rosecrans' opponent, General Braxton Bragg, was one of the most thoroughly disliked men in the Confederacy. Lieutenant Colonel James A. L. Fremantle, a visiting British officer who had met many of the South's generals, described Bragg in late spring of 1863 as the "least prepossessing" of them: tall and stooped and bright-eyed, but with "a sickly, cadaverous, haggard appearance, rather plain features, bushy black eyebrows which unite in a tuft on the top of his nose, and a stubby iron-gray beard."

Bragg's men resented their commander's harsh discipline, his officers questioned his competence and the general public despised him for his retreats. It was said that Bragg retreated whether he won or lost; a Confederate joke had it that he would never get to heaven because the moment he was invited to enter he would fall back.

Bragg's failures at the battles of Perryville and Stones River had so disgusted his subordinates that they were in a state of virtual revolt. His staunch friend, President Jefferson Davis, had been on the verge of removing him from command of his army.

The crisis had passed, but the sourness remained. Bragg had no illusions about how he stood with his corps and division commanders: They had told him, almost to a man, that they had no confidence in him and that he ought to be replaced. His enlisted men thought no better of their general. While riding near Tullahoma one day, Bragg asked a denim-clad man he saw on the road whether the fellow belonged to Bragg's army. "Bragg's got no army," the man snapped in reply. "He shot half of them himself in Kentucky, and the Yankees killed the other half of them up at Murfreesboro."

Thus it was a grim, irritable, contentious and sickly man who was preparing for yet another encounter with the Federal Army of the Cumberland.

Bragg prepared as best he could for the inevitable onslaught. Between his Duck River line and the Federals at Murfreesboro was a long ridge, extending southwest from the Cumberland Plateau. Four passes led through this mountain barrier: Guy's Gap on the far west, then Bellbuckle Gap, Liberty Gap and Hoover's Gap, farthest east. Hoover's Gap ran through mountainous country containing side roads ill suited for troop movements. The other three gaps were easier to negotiate and led directly toward

The death of General Earl Van Dorn at the hands of a jealous husband, Dr. George B. Peters, did not come as a great surprise to many of the general's fellow officers. Van Dorn was known to be an indefatigable ladies' man, and rumors had connected him with the doctor's beautiful wife, Jessie. "The General had great weakness in such matters," a fellow officer wrote; another bluntly termed Van Dorn "a horrible rake."

Bragg's lines. Bragg therefore placed his strength to his left, deploying Lieutenant General Leonidas Polk's corps, the largest, around Shelbyville in front of Guy's and Bellbuckle Gaps. Lieutenant General William Joseph Hardee held the right at Wartrace, eight miles east of Shelbyville, near Liberty Gap. It was also possible to approach Shelbyville from still farther west, by a roundabout route that avoided the ridge. Bragg was sure that such a move would appeal to Rosecrans, and so he sent most of Forrest's cavalry to range west of the ridge.

On the morning of June 24, as the Federal troops were marching out of Murfreesboro, rain began to fall. It fell steadily for the next 17 days — and "no Presbyterian rain, either," recalled one soldier, "but a genuine Baptist downpour." Roads turned to quagmires; an artilleryman said the guns in his unit traveled not on the roads but under

them. Major James A. Connolly, an officer in Wilder's brigade, recalled, "We lived in the rain, slept in the mud and rain, and were as wet as fish in the river."

The rain slowed, but did not halt, the Federal advance. And when the attack came on June 24, the Federals seemed to be everywhere at once. Rosecrans had devised an elaborate ruse in an effort to outsmart his opponent. He made the initial assault on the Confederate left as Bragg had anticipated; Major General David S. Stanley's cavalry swept around the end of the ridge and the Reserve Corps, commanded by Major General Gordon Granger, headed through Bellbuckle Gap down the road to Shelbyville. Away off to the Confederate right a lone Federal division was dispatched toward the town of McMinnville, so far to the east that it was beyond Hoover's Gap. When Bragg learned of the new Federal movement, he thought it clearly a feint intended to distract him from the main attack on Shelbyville.

In fact, the advance on Shelbyville was the feint. And the single division far to the east was part of Rosecrans' complicated deception: He intended Bragg to see it and take it for a decoy. But as Rosecrans had planned, the bulk of the Federal army was in motion not far behind this lone division. General Crittenden's XXI Corps was to follow it for a distance, punch through Forrest's cavalry screen up on the Cumberland Plateau, then drive south toward the town of Manchester, just 11 miles northeast of Tullahoma and well in the rear of the Confederate right. Meanwhile Major General George Henry Thomas with XIV Corps was to smash through Hoover's Gap, down the road that led directly to Manchester; and Major General Alexander McD. McCook's XX Corps, after marching a short distance toward Shelbyville to embellish the deception, would head through Liberty Gap straight for Hardee at Wartrace. If everything worked perfectly, Bragg's entire army might be cut off from its base at Chattanooga.

On June 24 McCook's corps encountered fierce resistance at Liberty Gap from a division led by Major General Patrick Cleburne, one of the Confederacy's finest soldiers and a man the Federals would get to know well in the coming days. It fell to General August Willich's brigade to clear the Confederates from the gap. But Willich's four regiments got nowhere against Cleburne's men. Deciding that a frontal attack was useless, Willich sent his men on a flanking movement around the Confederate defenders. Reinforced by two more regiments, Willich's troops clawed their way up the mountain on either side of the pass and eventually outflanked their en-

emy. Seeing the danger, Cleburne ordered a retreat, and the gap fell to the Federals.

But the heroes of the Federal assault on the gaps were the 1,500 mounted infantrymen of Wilder's brigade, who led General Thomas' corps down the main road toward Hoover's Gap. Wilder's inexperienced riders had received orders in the predawn drizzle of June 24 to trot into the gap, driving the enemy pickets ahead of them. Then the troopers were to wait for infantry support before attacking the Confederate fortifications across the narrowest part of the gap.

In fact, the Federal horsemen did not trot — they galloped. As the enemy pickets fled before them, the men of Wilder's brigade, spearheaded by the 72nd Indiana, gathered momentum. The advance was so swift that the Confederates had no time to organize any resistance. Before anyone quite knew it, Wilder's men were raging through the gap — at least 10 perilous miles ahead of their infantry support.

At that point, the Confederate forces began to collect themselves. Brigadier General William B. Bate's brigade, supported by that of Brigadier General Bushrod Johnson and three batteries of artillery, moved to intercept the Federals at the head of the gap. Encountering enemy shells, Wilder's men dismounted and formed a line of battle, supported by four guns of Captain Eli Lilly's 18th Indiana Battery. Lilly's gunners had kept up with the headlong race by galloping their horses; when at the last moment the animals gave out, the gunners hauled the guns into position by main force. Now it was the Confederates' turn to attack; the outnumbered Federals grimly prepared to stave off the two brigades as best they could.

Throughout the rainy afternoon of June

A crew of fugitive slaves recruited as laborers by General Rosecrans' army repairs a stretch of track near Murfreesboro, Tennessee, in 1863. Confederate raiders frequently tore up Rosecrans' vital supply line to Louisville. On one foray, John Hunt Morgan's horsemen destroyed bridges and trestles on more than 20 miles of the Louisville & Nashville main line.

24, Bate and Johnson tried repeatedly to dislodge Wilder from his position in the hills at the head of the gap. Time after time they were thrown back. So heavy was the Federal fire that General Bate believed he was facing a "vastly superior force." Major Connolly of Wilder's brigade recalled, "Our regiment lay on the hillside in mud and water, the rain pouring down in torrents, while each shell screamed so close to us as to make it seem that the next would tear us to pieces. Presently the enemy got near enough to us to make a charge on our battery, and on they came; our men are on their feet in an instant and a terrible fire from the Spencers causes the advancing regiment to reel and its colors fall to the ground."

The seven-shot Spencers carried by the Federal troopers were earning the enduring respect of both sides. Connolly would write to his wife: "Our men adore them as the heathen do their idols." Wilder's soldiers had sworn not to let any of the weapons fall into enemy hands. One fatally wounded soldier lacked the strength to smash his gun, said Connolly, "so he took out his knife, unscrewed a part of the lock plate and threw it away, rendering the gun entirely useless. He then fell back amid the storm of bullets, lay down and died."

During the afternoon Wilder was given a chance to withdraw. As Wilder remembered the incident, Major General John H. Reynolds, his division commander, sent an adjutant to order Wilder to retire from his exposed position. Wilder refused, insisting that he could hold on until Thomas' full corps, still six miles away, arrived. The adjutant threatened to arrest Wilder but then left when the brigade commander vowed to take full responsibility for his actions.

"We held our ground with continual fighting," Connolly wrote, "until 7 o'clock in the evening, when we discovered a battery coming up to our support as fast as the horses could run, and such a cheer as was sent up does one good to hear."

Wilder's men realized that if the artillery was on hand, the infantry could not be far behind. "We were nearly exhausted," Connolly related, "with the rapid march since before daylight in the morning, the continual rain, the half day's fighting, and nothing to eat since about two o'clock in the morning, yet the prospect of assistance nerved the men to maintain the unequal conflict a little longer." And sure enough, 30 minutes later two brigades of Reynolds' infantrymen arrived, worn out from their long, fast march. "We greeted them with such lusty cheers as seemed to inspire them with new vigor," Connolly said, "and they were soon in position; then came two more regiments of infantry, weary and footsore, but hurrying the best they could."

Soon General Thomas, the much-admired corps commander — a massive, rugged West Pointer who in 26 months of hard fighting had never led his men in a retreat — arrived. He grabbed Wilder's hand and declared: "You have saved the lives of a thousand men by your gallant conduct today. I didn't expect to get this gap for three days."

By nightfall the fighting died down. Remarkably, Federal casualties had been light, Wilder losing only 14 killed and 47 wounded. But the Spencers had taken a heavy toll of

Bivouacked on a farm in the Tennessee hills, officers and men of the 21st Michigan gather for a

photographer in the spring of 1863. Part of Philip Sheridan's division, the regiment, already tested at Stones River, would fight again at Chickamauga.

Confederates: Bate had lost 23 per cent of his force — 146 men killed or wounded.

At his headquarters in Tullahoma that night, Braxton Bragg was still trying to figure out what was happening. Confederate cavalry was reporting heavy Federal concentrations on the road to Shelbyville; there was no news from any of the gaps on the right.

All the next day, June 25, Bate and Johnson at Hoover's Gap and Cleburne at Liberty Gap struggled to regain possession of the two passes. The combative Cleburne launched a furious assault that pressed Willich's brigade back for a distance.

Sergeant Michael Bright of the 77th Pennsylvania recalled the fighting at Liberty Gap that afternoon: "The Rebels were drawn up in three lines on the Hill in front of us and their Artillery on the Right. In a very short time our regiment lost more than one fifth of its men in killed and wounded." The 77th Pennsylvania was almost out of ammunition when at last two Federal regiments came up and helped drive Cleburne's force back.

It was not until the following day, however, that Bragg at last became aware of the heavy fighting on his right and hastily shifted his focus to what he now thought had become the main battleground. By the afternoon of the 26th, Polk, who had been holding Shelbyville, was getting ready to rush to Cleburne's assistance at Liberty Gap.

Finally, on the evening of June 26, when he had been under attack for almost three days, a dismayed Bragg suddenly realized the full extent of his danger. That day Wilder's brigade — now coming to be known among Federal soldiers as the Lightning Brigade for its swift occupation of Hoover's Gap — broke through the Confederates and led Thomas' corps southward toward Man-

lonel John T. Wilder, commander
the Federal mounted brigade, not
ly had to find mounts and weapons
r his former infantrymen but also
is obliged to teach them how to
re for the animals. "At the begin-
ng we were perfectly green at it,"
e of his soldiers admitted; "the
en never thought about feeding or
rrying their horses."

chester. When Bragg learned that a Federal force was in position to cut him off from Chattanooga, he sent urgent orders for both Polk and Hardee to fall back to Tullahoma.

The rain continued, adding to the Confederates' misery. In Tullahoma, Captain Irving A. Buck of the 17th Virginia reported that some soldiers lost their shoes in the mire—in the middle of town. A mule, he said, had been seen "to fall and suffocate in the mud of the streets." When a drenched member of Hardee's staff was asked the derivation of the town's name, he said sourly that it came from two Greek words: *tulla,* meaning "mud," and *homa,* meaning "more mud."

The mud was little deterrent to the Federals. Wilder's horsemen splashed into Manchester at a gallop on the morning of June 27. That afternoon the rest of the corps arrived, and early the next morning Wilder's men were on the move again. Hurrying southward in the rain, occasionally swimming the

swollen rivers on horseback, that night they reached Decherd, a junction on the Nashville & Chattanooga Railroad. And there they did telling damage: They wrecked a railroad trestle, tore up track, and destroyed supplies and equipment before prudently retiring in the face of a strong Confederate force. Although the damage was soon repaired, for a time Bragg's communications with Chattanooga were out.

On the night of June 29 at Tullahoma, a perplexed and indecisive Bragg met with his top commanders to discuss what they should do. The Confederates were now concentrated at Tullahoma; but Rosecrans, instead of attacking, was quite evidently trying to get behind Bragg by way of Manchester. The Confederate commander received little help from his two corps leaders. Polk urged retreat. Hardee was not sure, but he seemed inclined to stay and fight. Bragg's council of war broke up without reaching a decision.

A detachment of Colonel Wilder's mounted brigade, with fast-firing Spencer rifles slung at their sides, rides past an outpost designed to protect the Nashville & Chattanooga tracks from Confederate raiders. "Our brigade is evidently regarded as a useful appendage to this army," one of Wilder's officers wrote home, "for either the entire brigade or a portion of it is in use almost constantly."

The next day, June 30, Bragg's situation deteriorated so swiftly that a decision was forced on him. The three Federal corps of Thomas, McCook and Crittenden had reached Manchester; and although their men were exhausted by the long march through the mud, they began closing in on Bragg from the northeast. Granger's Reserve Corps and some of Stanley's cavalry had taken Shelbyville the previous day. Bragg feared that he was about to be caught in a trap. That night, he ordered the Confederates to abandon Tullahoma and fall back south of the Elk River near Decherd to make a stand. Bragg's troops reached the Elk the next day, July 1, but remained there for only a few hours. Increasingly concerned that Rosecrans would succeed in flanking him, Bragg resumed his retreat east into the mountains and across the broad Tennessee River to Chattanooga.

General Rosecrans arrived in Tullahoma on July 3. His nine-day campaign had been a model of planning and execution, but he had the misfortune of consummating his triumph at the wrong time. July 4 brought the two greatest Federal victories of the War to date, at Gettysburg and Vicksburg. Amid the rejoicing over those triumphs in the North, the fall of tiny Tullahoma received scant attention. Yet it was an event of great importance. The Confederates had been all but swept from Tennessee at a cost of 84 Federal dead and 476 wounded, captured or missing. Total Confederate losses were never reported, but they were much higher.

Once again Bragg had got his army away, but as he rode grimly into the Tennessee mountains he was under no illusions about his withdrawal. When Bishop Charles Quintard, the chaplain of the 1st Tennessee, called out from the side of the road that Bragg seemed exhausted, the general reined in his horse for a moment, and said: "Yes, I am utterly broken down." Then he leaned over the saddle and told the clergyman in a hoarse whisper, "This is a great disaster."

The truce between Rosecrans and his superiors in Washington, produced by his success at Tullahoma, lasted only three days. On July 7, General Rosecrans was stung by a gratuitous communication from the Secretary of War, Edwin M. Stanton: "Lee's army overthrown; Grant victorious. You and your noble army now have the chance to give the finishing blow to the rebellion. Will you neglect the chance?"

Rosecrans' reply was immediate and scathing. "You do not appear to observe the fact that this noble army" — the sarcastic use of Stanton's own words cannot have escaped the Secretary's attention — "has driven the rebels from Middle Tennessee. I beg in behalf of this army that the War Department may not overlook so great an event because it is not written in letters of blood."

That set the tone for the communications that followed; Stanton remained insistent, Rosecrans adamant. Again, Rosecrans refused to move until he was ready. As usual, he had his reasons, and they were not frivolous. He was being asked to pursue Bragg into mountainous country and across a great river. It would be hard to supply his army in such terrain and at such a distance from his Nashville base. The railroad that must carry his rations and ammunition was partially wrecked and needed repairs.

Moreover, Rosecrans felt that if he were to thrust deep into enemy country, he must have protection on his flanks. He regarded General Joseph E. Johnston, whose army

Hurrying along the road through Hoover's Gap and storming up the nearby hills, the main body of General George Thomas' corps follows Wilder's mounted brigade through the vital pass on June 24, 1863. The scene was depicted by a self-taught watercolorist named Horace Rawdon, a soldier in the 105th Ohio.

Hoovers Gap

had been driven by Grant into Mississippi, as a threat to his right; Rosecrans proposed that Grant be ordered to watch Johnston. The response was a single, curt sentence from Halleck: "Grant's movements at present have no connection with you."

Rosecrans' superiors did, however, share his concern about his left flank. In Knoxville, just a little more than 100 miles to the northeast of Chattanooga, the Confederates had stationed a small force under Major General Simon Bolivar Buckner. General Bragg

had already summoned Buckner to Chattanooga, and he was on the way with half of his forces. But there was another, more compelling reason for Washington officials to worry about northeastern Tennessee.

The region around Knoxville had concerned President Lincoln since the earliest days of the War. Although it was in Confederate hands, its population—mainly small farmers with little enthusiasm for slavery—was strongly Unionist. These people, a Federal officer wrote, "were hunted by rebel mobs and proscribed by rebel authorities, were persecuted and driven to caves, imprisoned, starved, tortured, put to death. It was a sacred duty of the government to go to the rescue of these people."

That duty had been delegated to Major General Ambrose E. Burnside, who had presided in December over the disastrous Federal attack on Fredericksburg. Relieved of command of the 114,000-man Army of the Potomac, he had in March been given command of the 24,000-man Army of the Ohio, stationed near Cincinnati. His job was to drive across northern Tennessee and run the Confederates out of Knoxville, meanwhile protecting the left flank of Rosecrans' army.

Burnside had been preparing to move when his IX Corps had been taken from him to assist in the siege of Vicksburg; he was awaiting its return before advancing, although the force opposing him was even smaller than his reduced Army of the Ohio.

Halleck now had to goad two generals instead of only one. "Burnside has been frequently urged to move forward and cover your left," he said in a testy telegram to Rosecrans. "I do not know what he is doing. He seems tied fast to Cincinnati."

At last Halleck lost patience. On August 4 he sent an unequivocal message to Rosecrans. "Your forces," he said, "must move forward without further delay. You will daily report the movement of each corps until you cross the Tennessee River." A similar notice was sent to Burnside. Rosecrans, incredulous, requested confirmation. "The orders," replied Halleck, "are peremptory."

Still more time passed. But finally, on August 16, both the Army of the Cumberland and the Army of the Ohio began to move toward the Confederates. Rosecrans had been camped in Tullahoma for six weeks.

As usual, once he got started, Rosecrans moved with the easy footwork and confidence of a fine boxer. Again his target was the Confederate line of communications. And again he caught Bragg off guard.

Rosecrans had studied the topography around Chattanooga with great care. The easiest approach to the city from the west was the valley of the Tennessee River. But it was also easily defended. The mountainous terrain on both sides of the valley would play a decisive role in the struggle for Chattanooga.

North of the river rose a great mountain, Walden's Ridge. To the south, in Georgia, a series of mountain ranges extended like fingers, pointing toward Chattanooga from the southwest. These were Raccoon Mountain to the west, Lookout Mountain in the middle — the most imposing, rising more than 2,000 feet above sea level and extending 30 miles — then Missionary Ridge and Pigeon Mountain on the east. The ranges were extremely difficult to cross. They were broken by passes, but the passes were steep and the roads through them were poor — some of them mere footpaths. The valleys between these hills were narrow and uninviting, with one exception; between Missionary Ridge and Pigeon Mountain lay a wide, fertile bowl known locally as McLemore's Cove.

Of all the options open to Rosecrans, the most attractive — and the course Bragg expected him to take — was an approach from the north, across the towering mass of Walden's Ridge. That route not only gave direct access to Chattanooga but led in one easy step to Bragg's communication line — the vital railroad junction east of the city. Moreover, since Burnside would be somewhere on the north side of Chattanooga, Rosecrans could more easily join forces with him.

Yet after studying his maps, Rosecrans decided to cross the river and approach Chattanooga from the southwest. At first glance the route seemed to have little to recommend it. There were only two passages leading eastward through Lookout Mountain, and they were some miles distant from Chattanooga. Worse, to get the Federal army rapidly into position, both of these passes, plus a rail-and-road route up the Tennessee River valley past Lookout Mountain, would have to be used at the same time — and the various units would be dangerously divided.

Although the southern route was by far the trickier option, it had two great advantages. The first was that the Federal forces would be closer to their supply line, the Nashville & Chattanooga Railroad, which joined the Memphis and Charleston road at Stevenson, southwest of Chattanooga. Second, and more important, the mere presence of Federal troops in the mountains below Chattanooga would pose an intolerable threat to Bragg's communications along the Western & Atlantic Railroad to Atlanta, and Bragg might well be forced to evacuate the town to protect the rail line.

On August 16 the complex Federal movement toward Chattanooga began. With Crittenden's corps on the left, Thomas' in the center and McCook's on the right, 50,000 infantrymen advanced on a 50-mile front, screened by 9,000 cavalrymen and supported by 200 guns — and Bragg was completely unaware of the approaching Federals.

To keep Bragg in the dark, Rosecrans assigned three infantry brigades under Brigadier General William B. Hazen, strongly supported by cavalry, to feint toward Chattanooga from the north. In the vanguard, yet again, rode the fast-firing troopers of John T. Wilder's Lightning Brigade.

Wilder's force rode out of Tullahoma and headed east into the rugged mountains, later to turn toward Chattanooga. "We shall keep in the obscure trails and hope to surprise the place," James Connolly of Wilder's brigade wrote home. And indeed, the troopers captured a remarkable number of Confederates as they advanced. Even though Bragg was expecting an attack from the north, his cavalry was not on guard and his troops were being taken unawares.

Friday, August 21, had been one of those days that Jefferson Davis occasionally set aside for prayer and fasting throughout the Confederacy, and in Chattanooga civilians and soldiers alike flocked to the churches. The roads to the city were barely guarded; no one suspected that there were Federals nearby. Suddenly, at 9 a.m., from the main ferry station on the north bank of the Tennessee River, Wilder's battery under Eli Lilly opened fire on the town across the river with stunning effect; Henry Campbell, bugler of the 18th Indiana Artillery, reported that the worshippers at one church "poured out like bees from a hive." Civilians began to flee the town. A boat at the unguarded ferry slip on the south bank was sunk by the artillery fire, and a number of shells exploded inside Confederate fortifications, which were clearly visible from the opposite bank.

Although Hazen's forces were not strong enough to storm the town, for almost three weeks they stayed in the vicinity, harassing its defenders. At night, fires were lit along the roads near the town to make it appear that a large body of men was gathering. It was Rosecrans' favorite ploy; he had used it before at Stones River. The Federals also noisily clapped boards together, pounded barrels and threw wood scraps into the river to give the impression that boats were being constructed for a crossing.

By August 21, Bragg knew from scouting reports that the bulk of the Federal army was moving toward him, but he had no idea where the main force was. His army, plagued by illness and desertions, now totaled only about 30,000 men. Bragg pleaded with Richmond for reinforcements and was promised 20,000 men — some from Johnston in Mississippi, and more from Robert E. Lee's Army of Northern Virginia.

Bragg had his army deployed to fight off an attack from the north — Polk's corps in Chattanooga, Hardee's a short distance to the northeast, where it could interpose itself between Rosecrans and Burnside. Now word reached the Confederates that Burnside was heading for Knoxville with 15,000 men. Buckner had left only about 2,500 men in the Knoxville area and they were no match for Burnside; Bragg pulled the little unit out of Knoxville and back toward Chattanooga to bolster his own defense.

Amid all this, General Hardee was suddenly transferred to Mississippi to help Johnston, whose army had been dwindling as a result of desertions and unauthorized furloughs. Hardee, a good organizer, was assigned to round up the stragglers and reconstitute Johnston's forces. To replace him, President Davis promoted Major General Daniel Harvey Hill to lieutenant general and sent him west. Hill was a difficult and moody man, but he was an old friend of Bragg's; they had been Army messmates in Texas in 1845 during the Mexican War. It must have seemed to Davis that Bragg, surrounded for so long by discontented subordinates, would benefit from having a friend at his side. But it was not to be. Hill viewed Bragg as a changed man. "He had grown prematurely old since I saw him last," wrote Hill, "and showed much nervousness." Their meeting, he said, was "not satisfactory."

Bragg had ample reason for nervousness. He was getting reports of Federal advances that seemed to be coming from all over the map, and it was critical that he divine the real threat. "It is said to be easy to defend a mountainous country," he said querulously to Hill, "but mountains hide your foe from you, while they are full of gaps through which he can pounce on you at any time. A mountain is like the wall of a house full of rat holes. The rat lies hidden at his hole, ready to pop out when no one is watching."

It seemed likely that Bragg was looking at the right wall — that is, north of Chattanooga. All during the last week of August he received reports of Federal activity in that area. There were also fragmentary accounts of a Federal presence around the town of Stevenson, to the southwest, but these did not seem significant.

Then, on August 31, a Confederate sympathizer reported that a powerful force was crossing the river at Stevenson and pouring into the mountains south of Chattanooga. The next morning, one of Wheeler's cavalry patrols confirmed the civilian's report. Yet Bragg dared not shift large numbers of men away from the northern approaches to the city while there was still a chance that the attack might come from that direction. He vacillated. He shifted a few units. For a whole week the Confederate commanders sifted through their scanty reports and tried to figure out which of them to believe. Three times Bragg started to pull out of Chat-

Braxton Bragg's notoriously short temper was the result, some believed, of the general's chronic ill health and penchant for overwork. "He was frequently in the saddle," one noted, "when the more appropriate place for him would have been in bed."

tanooga, and each time reversed himself.

At last, the evidence was irrefutable. Rosecrans was unquestionably in the Confederates' rear with large numbers of troops. Just as had happened at Tullahoma, Bragg had been outmaneuvered, his communications were being threatened, and he had to move his army southward or risk being cut off. Late on September 7 the Confederates gave up Chattanooga, the great prize of the West, without firing a shot, and marched over the dusty roads leading south.

Rosecrans was exultant. On the morning of September 9 he telegraphed Halleck: "Chattanooga is ours without a struggle and East Tennessee is free." Then he sent his entire army marching at full speed after Bragg. Thomas Crittenden and his XXI Corps were to move up the Tennessee River valley into Chattanooga and then follow Bragg's line of retreat. Alexander McCook and XX Corps were sent far to the south, 50 miles below Chattanooga, with orders to get behind the Confederate army if possible; they would cross Lookout via the more distant of its passes, Winston's Gap, and push east. George Thomas and XIV Corps were sent charging eastward through the middle route, via Stevens' Gap and McLemore's Cove. Thomas' orders were to "strike the enemy in flank, and if possible cut off his escape."

Before taking to the road, Thomas, a general who rarely questioned an order, made a suggestion to the suddenly adventurous Rosecrans. Instead of separating the three corps, he said, it might be prudent to consolidate the position around Chattanooga before chasing Bragg. The city could then serve as a secure base for the offensive.

Rosecrans brushed aside Thomas' proposal. Bragg was fleeing for his life, and here was a golden opportunity to destroy him. The commanding general was full of optimism and high spirits. Major Connolly wrote to his wife: "Rosecrans told General Reynolds yesterday that he didn't expect to get a fight out of Bragg this side of Atlanta."

There was plenty of evidence that Bragg was in disarray. As the Federals had neared Chattanooga, captured and deserting Confederates reported that the Army of Tennessee was in full flight, headed into Georgia toward Rome and Atlanta. The mountain people along Bragg's route gave a similar account: Confederate officers were admitting that their army was in panicky retreat.

But strangely, as the Federals continued to race ahead, they saw increasingly ominous signs of the enemy all around those finger-like mountains. Thomas was running into unexpected pockets of Confederate opposition. General Beatty, with Thomas' vanguard in McLemore's Cove, remarked nervously in his diary that "information poured in upon us from all quarters that the enemy, in strength, was making dispositions to surround and cut us off before reinforcements could arrive." And that was exactly what the enemy had been planning.

Bragg was not in full-scale retreat. His withdrawal had been orderly, and he had stopped on September 9 near Chattanooga in the vicinity of La Fayette, across Pigeon Mountain from McLemore's Cove. The sto-

Federal troops and wagons cross a pontoon bridge spanning the Tennessee River at Caperton's Ferry, about 25 miles southwest of Chattanooga, during Rosecrans' bold attempt to outflank Bragg's army. The artist, William Travis, portrayed Rosecrans pointing his sword at left.

ries of panicky flight had been cleverly orchestrated — Rosecrans was not the only general playing such games. The deserters pouring out their tales of demoralization had been sent to the unwary Federals by Bragg. The local civilians had been carefully misled by well-briefed Confederate officers.

Moreover, Bragg had taken the time to reshuffle his infantry units into a new organization of four corps, each with two divisions. In addition to Polk and Hill, the corps commanders were Buckner and Major General William H. T. Walker, who had just come from Mississippi. Bragg's men, wrote Captain Irving Buck, were eager, enthusiastic and "in fine condition." Bragg's reinforcements were beginning to arrive, and soon his

troops would outnumber those of Rosecrans.

Moreover, Bragg knew where Thomas' corps was. He had kept the Federal forces under almost constant surveillance as they marched through the hills.

In fact, Thomas and his 20,000 men were marching into a trap in McLemore's Cove. On its south end, where Missionary Ridge and Pigeon Mountain converged, the valley was a cul de sac. The Confederates were blocking the passes leading eastward through Pigeon Mountain with felled trees and guarding them with infantry and artillery. And the broad northern mouth of the valley was rapidly filling with Confederate troops — which would number 23,000 in all.

On the evening of September 9, Bragg

After crossing the Tennessee River, Federal soldiers and supply wagons struggle from Hog Jaw Valley up the rugged flank of Lookout Mountain. That ridge and Raccoon and Sand Mountains slowed the Federal advance to a crawl. "Roads horrible," one of Thomas' division commanders reported to Rosecrans; "fully as bad as anything we have had."

General James Scott Negley stands bareheaded in front of his staff on a steep mountain slope a few days before his division led Thomas' XIV Corps into the valley called McLemore's Cove. Negley was worried that he might have fallen into a trap. "There are indications of a superior force of the enemy being in position near Dug Gap," he reported from McLemore's Cove. "My position is somewhat advanced and exposed."

sent orders for the trap to be sprung the next morning; one of Polk's divisions under Major General Thomas C. Hindman, recently arrived from Arkansas, was to move south into McLemore's Cove. There he was to smash into Thomas' lead division, commanded by Major General James S. Negley. Meanwhile, one of D. H. Hill's divisions, led by General Cleburne, was to march west from La Fayette through one of the gaps in Pigeon Mountain to join in the assault.

The plan was good enough, but on the morning of the 10th, things began to go wrong for the Confederates. When Hindman was partway into the valley, he began to fret that Hill might be delayed in getting through

the gap. Hindman decided it would be more prudent to delay his attack until he was certain that Hill was on the scene.

And, to be sure, Hill's division had encountered delays. To begin with, for some reason Bragg's order to Hill took five hours to reach him. When Hill finally got the order, it was nearly dawn and he thought of a long list of reasons for not obeying: He claimed that Cleburne was ailing and that his troops were out of position; the barricades that the Confederates had erected in the gaps to block the Federals now had to be removed and this would take time; Thomas might himself be setting a trap. Hill listed these excuses in a querulous message to Bragg that took more than three hours to reach its destination. Nothing happened. Bragg was frantic. Captain Buck saw him pacing back and forth as he awaited the sounds of battle; "occasionally he would stop and irritably dig his spurs into the ground."

At last on the afternoon of the 10th Bragg desperately sent one of Buckner's divisions to bolster Hindman. But when Buckner and Hindman met around 8 p.m., they held a council of war, solemnly discussed the situation and decided to do nothing. Although Bragg again ordered Hindman to attack, Hindman stayed where he was; he did promise to attack the next morning, however.

But before anything could happen on the 11th, the Federals made a crucial move. Negley, like his brigade commander John Beatty, was seeing signs of the enemy; to play it safe, he pulled back to Stevens' Gap, through which he had entered McLemore's Cove — and now his only escape route. The Confederate opportunity was lost.

In the early-morning hours of September 12, Bragg made another effort to snare a Federal corps — this time Crittenden's force, which was marching southward from Chattanooga right into the heart of the Confederate army. Crittenden had sent Brigadier General Thomas J. Wood's division ahead while he proceeded to the railroad town of Ringgold with his remaining two divisions. Wood pushed all the way to the mouth of McLemore's Cove, to a place called Lee and Gordon's Mill. There, Wood's division was only about 15 miles north of La Fayette, Bragg's headquarters — and almost that far by road from the rest of Crittenden's corps at Ringgold. Wood was perilously isolated and so close to the Confederates that, unknowingly, he almost collided with Hindman.

Bragg knew of Wood's presence and he saw yet another chance to strike a crippling blow. As a first step, he ordered Polk to attack Wood. Crush that division, Bragg told Polk, "and the others are yours." But because of faulty intelligence, Bragg sent Polk to the wrong place to make the attack on Wood. And by the time Polk had found the enemy the odds had changed: Crittenden was moving with his other two divisions from Ringgold to join Wood at Lee and Gordon's Mill. Now Polk decided that he was dangerously outnumbered. In fact, the reverse was true — Polk had four divisions to send against Crittenden's three, and Bragg was prepared to send him more. Nevertheless, there were now more troops facing Polk than he had been led to expect, and he decided not to attack. Crittenden, meanwhile, withdrew north for a distance, and Bragg, uncertain, fell back toward La Fayette.

Bragg raged, but nothing could be done to retrieve his fumbled opportunities. His officers would later contend that Bragg's orders had been vague, uninformed, and discretionary. General Hill wrote that Bragg had issued "impossible orders, and therefore those entrusted with their execution got in the way of disregarding them." Moreover, Hill recorded, Bragg had earned such a reputation for finding "a scapegoat for every failure and disaster" that his subordinates were all reluctant to take the initiative.

At any rate, the Confederates had no monopoly on ineptitude during this period of fruitless maneuvering. Rosecrans had been told repeatedly that Bragg was standing fast; he simply did not believe it. After Negley had recoiled from McLemore's Cove on September 11, Thomas, his superior, had swiftly reported the presence there of the enemy;

**OFFICER'S
DRESS SHIRT**

A Valiant Officer's Sartorial Legacy

Very few uniforms survived the Civil War intact. One of the rare exceptions, shown here, was proudly preserved by a Mississippi infantry officer, T. Otis Baker, who fought with Braxton Bragg's army in Tennessee and earned a citation for "conspicuous bravery" at Chickamauga. Despite suffering three wounds, Baker continued to serve the Confederacy until the War's end.

Lieutenant Baker's butternut-colored frock coat and trousers are made of homespun wool, reflecting the fact that in the western armies both officers and men had to make do with simple, locally produced fabrics — in contrast to the gray uniforms of finer cloth worn by officers in the East. Similarly, Baker's inelegant slouch hat is of rough, brown wool felt, and his sword is also a local product, made at the small forge operated by A. H. Dewitt in Columbus, Georgia.

By contrast, Baker's shirt boasts an elaborate pattern that was popular among the best-dressed Confederate officers. No gentleman of the era went without a jacket on any occasion — unless he wore a fancy shirt. Baker's is trimmed with an ornamental collar, a yoke and cuffs of blue silk.

STRIPED SUSPENDERS

HOMESPUN TROUSERS

SWORD AND SCABBARD

PREWAR PHOTOGRAPH OF T. OTIS BAKER
AND HIS WIFE

HAT OF WOOL FELT

FROCK COAT WITH SECOND
LIEUTENANT'S SLEEVE BRAID AND RANK
BAR (REAR VIEW AT RIGHT)

OFFICER'S DISPATCH CASE

and a few hours later he added, "All information goes to confirm that a large part of Bragg's army is opposed to Negley." Rosecrans replied in a jaunty wire: "Your dispatches of 10:30 last night and again of 4 this morning have been received. After maturely weighing the notes, the general commanding is induced to think that General Negley withdrew more through prudence than compulsion. He trusts that our loss is not serious."

But evidence of large Confederate deployments in the immediate area continued to mount. Far to the south General McCook reported hearing that "Bragg's whole army," along with part of Johnston's, was at La Fayette. And once more Negley reported in: He had seen clouds of dust in the Dug Gap area of Pigeon Mountain, indicating the movements of large Confederate units.

The signs were unmistakable — and by September 13, at last, Rosecrans saw that his scattered corps were in grave danger. Pulling his forces together had become, he now acknowledged, "a matter of life and death."

He ordered Thomas to shift his troops from Stevens' Gap to Pond Spring, a position just five miles from Crittenden's corps around Lee and Gordon's Mill. McCook, perilously exposed about 30 miles to the south at a town called Alpine, was also summoned northward. McCook laboriously retraced his steps westward across Lookout Mountain, up the valley west of it and then back eastward across the mountain to where Thomas had been camped in Stevens' Gap. It was a painful 57-mile march — "extremely exhausting," said Major General Philip Sheridan, one of McCook's division commanders. The supply wagons and artillery had to be dragged up the mountain roads and inched down again by manpower; the troops

made forced marches of as much as 25 miles a day. In all, the long trip back took more than four days. Rosecrans waited apprehensively, but Bragg did nothing.

By September 17, Rosecrans was able to breathe easily again. His army was closing up near Lee and Gordon's Mill. The risk of being defeated one corps at a time had passed. But the threat of attack was far from ended.

For days there had been rumors that Bragg was being reinforced. Now it was all coming true. In addition to Buckner's men, troops from Johnston had arrived; and a corps under Lee's best commander, Lieutenant General James Longstreet, would be on the scene within a few days. The leading elements of Longstreet's 12,000-man force were already in Georgia, steaming toward Chattanooga as fast as the battered Confederate rail system could take them. They were the cream of Lee's army; "no better troops could be found anywhere," commented one of Lee's staff officers, Colonel Walter H. Taylor, as he watched them entrain.

Originally the corps was to have traveled straight across Virginia to Knoxville and then to Chattanooga, a trip that might have been managed in two days. But then Burnside had captured Knoxville. Denied the direct route, Longstreet's men had to make their way down through the Carolinas and across Georgia, a distance of more than 900 miles. They used no fewer than 16 railroads — and railroads of differing gauges, so that the soldiers frequently had to change trains when they came to a new line.

Longstreet's troops were traveling light; General John Bell Hood — his crippled left arm still in a sling from a serious wound received at Gettysburg — commented that the men "were destitute of almost everything, I

General William Rosecrans, sitting in front of a tree, is flanked by members of his staff, including his chief of staff Brigadier General James A. Garfield (*seated, right, next to Rosecrans*). One of Rosecrans' most skilled division commanders, Major General Philip Sheridan, sits at far right.

might say, except pride, spirit, and forty rounds of ammunition to the man.'' They did, however, have something rare in the Confederacy: new uniforms, supplied by Governor Zebulon Vance from North Carolina mills. Curiously, the new clothes were blue and, except for the tight cut, resembled the standard Union uniforms.

On September 15 Halleck informed Rosecrans that Longstreet was headed for Chattanooga and began at once to shift troops to Rosecrans from Grant and other commands. At the same time Rosecrans also pressed for reinforcements; ''At least, push Burnside down,'' he urged Halleck.

But Rosecrans would not soon see help from Burnside, and it was his own fault. On September 10 he had sent word to Burnside that Bragg was fleeing deep into Georgia; he

had asked Burnside for cavalry only. Burnside had sent the cavalry and then made plans to push eastward into Virginia, where the Confederates had valuable salt works. Thus as Longstreet's troops swelled the enemy army confronting Rosecrans south of Chattanooga, Burnside notified President Lincoln that he was proceeding eastward toward the little town of Jonesboro, Tennessee — whereupon the exasperated President, deeply concerned about the fate of the Army of the Cumberland, exploded with a rare bit of profanity. ''Damn Jonesboro!'' he cried, and wired Burnside to hurry southward.

But there was no time left. Below Chattanooga, the two armies were lying too close together to avoid contact, separated only by a little stream the Cherokees had called the River of Blood, or Chickamauga.

River of Blood

"The army is simply a mob. There appears to be neither organization nor discipline. Were a division of the enemy to pounce down upon us, I fear the Army of the Cumberland would be blotted out of existence."

BRIGADIER GENERAL JOHN BEATTY, U.S.A., AFTER THE BATTLE OF CHICKAMAUGA

2

On September 18, Braxton Bragg, his fighting blood still aroused, again ordered a Confederate attack, this time against General Crittenden's XXI Corps at Lee and Gordon's Mill. Bragg hoped to get his troops in motion quickly, turn Crittenden's left and then attack him frontally, driving the Federal corps into McLemore's Cove, penning the force in and destroying it. In doing so, he would also cut Rosecrans' line of retreat to Chattanooga. This time Bragg's orders were unmistakably peremptory, closing with the words: "The movement will be executed with the utmost promptness, vigor and persistence."

For all Bragg's determination, everything went wrong that day. Before the Confederates could attack, they had to get across Chickamauga Creek. Despite Bragg's demand for speed, all three of the units he had chosen to lead the turning movement were late getting to their crossing points.

Bushrod Johnson's division was to attack across Reed's Bridge on the Confederate right; he would be joined later by Major General John B. Hood, with the first of Longstreet's units to arrive from Virginia. But Johnson, following orders he had received earlier, was heading in the wrong direction when his new instructions came and had to countermarch for several miles. Walker's corps was to take the center, with Buckner's to the left. They were also a long way from their crossing points, and they had both been routed for a time over the same narrow dirt road. Buckner reached Thedford's Ford at

2 p.m., brushing aside the Federal pickets; but he received no word from Walker, to his right. Uneasy, he waited awhile. Then he bivouacked for the night, after having crossed only a part of his force to the west bank of Chickamauga Creek.

The other two generals found the bridges by which they were to cross defended by Federal horsemen. When Johnson's division reached Reed's Bridge, it was stopped there by a Federal cavalry brigade commanded by Irish-born Colonel Robert H. G. Minty. And Walker's men found themselves in a vicious fight at Alexander's Bridge with John Wilder's ubiquitous Lightning Brigade. The Federal troopers inflicted 105 casualties among Walker's Confederates with the loss of only one man; but the Lightning Brigade was outnumbered and eventually had to retire. Before they withdrew, Wilder's men removed the decking from the bridge; Walker's force had to wade the creek at Lambert's Ford more than a mile to the north.

Late in the afternoon General Hood and his three brigades joined Johnson's division at Reed's Bridge. Many of Hood's soldiers had come on a different train from his and had not seen their general since Gettysburg. There was a brief, joyous reunion—Hood was one of the Confederacy's most popular commanders—and then he led his men in a triumphant attack across the bridge that drove back Minty's Federal troopers.

By the end of the day Bragg had only a small part of his force—fewer than 9,000

Discovered at Chickamauga in the 1880s, this brass eagle topped the flagstaff of one of the Federal regiments that fought under Major General George H. Thomas during the desperate defense of Horseshoe Ridge on the second day of the battle. Seven skulls were found scattered near the eagle, testifying to the gallant resistance of the color guard before they were overwhelmed by the onrushing Confederates.

men — across the Chickamauga. But the Confederates continued to cross all night, and by morning almost three quarters of the army was aligned on the thickly forested west bank, ready at last to attack.

But Rosecrans was ready, too. On the night of the 17th, unbeknownst to Bragg, Rosecrans had ordered Crittenden to extend his left to prevent just the kind of attack Bragg was planning. Rosecrans continued to worry about his left during the 18th as he watched the dust clouds raised by the Confederate movements, and that night he ordered General Thomas to march XIV Corps around Crittenden to the north. By dawn, two of Thomas' divisions — those under Brigadier Generals John M. Brannan and Absalom Baird — were in position while those of Reynolds and Negley were still on the march northward.

Bragg thought the Federal left was still around Lee and Gordon's Mill. In fact, by the morning of September 19 it had moved three and a half miles to the north, and Bragg's flanking movement was itself overlapped by the new Federal line. Rosecrans, just as uninformed, did not know that most of Bragg's army was on his side of the creek.

Despite all of Bragg's efforts to be the aggressor, the opening shots were fired by Federal troops. After fighting at Reed's Bridge on September 18, Colonel Dan McCook, the 29-year-old brother of the Federal XX Corps commander, told General Thomas that an enemy brigade had crossed the creek. Early on the 19th Thomas ordered General Brannan, on the extreme left of the XIV Corps line, to attack the lone Confederate unit.

Brannan sent the brigade of Colonel John T. Croxton in the direction of the bridge. On the way, about 8 a.m., Croxton's men encountered Forrest's Confederate cavalry and opened fire. "Our tremendous volley rang along the whole line," wrote Private T. B. Kellenberger of the 6th Indiana. "At first all was smoke, then dust from the struggling steeds. A few riderless horses were running here and there, save which nothing was seen of that cavalry troop. Thus began the Battle of Chickamauga."

Croxton was driving Forrest back toward the creek when a division of Walker's corps, under Brigadier General States Rights Gist — a 32-year-old South Carolinian whose name reflected his father's secessionist ideology — smashed into the astonished Federals with terrific force. Despite his mortal peril, Croxton retained his sense of humor and sent a wry message back to Thomas: Which Rebel brigade was he supposed to capture?

Brannan hurried the rest of his division to the assistance of Croxton and was soon heavily engaged with Gist's Confederates. It quickly became apparent that there were more Confederates than a Federal division, let alone a single brigade, could handle. "The enemy bore down upon Brannan like a mountain torrent," wrote the correspondent of the Chicago *Journal*, "sweeping away a brigade as if it had been driftwood."

Thomas rushed up Baird's division, and the Federal lines steadied. Walker thereupon countered with another Confederate division, led by Brigadier General St. John Liddell. Again the Confederates drove the Federals from their lines, pushing Brannan and Baird all the way back to their starting point. Among Liddell's trophies were five of the six guns in Lieutenant George Van Pelt's 1st Michigan Battery. When his infantry support gave way Van Pelt had stood fast,

pouring 64 rounds of canister into the charging ranks of the 8th Arkansas. But the onslaught was overwhelming; Van Pelt was killed and his battery captured.

As the Federal troops gave ground, Thomas called on Rosecrans for help. Negley and Reynolds had not yet arrived, and Thomas missed them sorely. Rosecrans immediately sent General Richard Johnson's division from Alexander McCook's corps. As these fresh troops advanced they met a large body of Federal soldiers falling back. The newcomers coolly broke formation by companies "to let the retreating crowds pass through," in the words of one officer, then re-formed and continued their march. In a moment they were in the midst of the seesaw melee. Now it was the Confederates' turn to retreat. Walker called for help, and soon Major General Benjamin F. Cheatham's division was marching to his support.

The battle, stoked steadily by reinforce-

ments, increased in fury, and the din became unearthly. One of Forrest's cavalry officers, Colonel Thomas Berry, recorded his impressions: "Neighing horses, wild and frightened, were running in every direction; whistling, seething, crackling bullets, the piercing, screaming fragments of shells, the whirring sound of shrapnel and the savage shower of canister, mingled with the fierce answering yells of defiance, all united in one horrible sound."

Berry wrote that he had been in numerous battles and had never seen one so awful. "The ghastly, mangled dead and horribly wounded strewed the earth for over half a mile up and down the river banks," he reported. "The dead were piled upon each other in ricks, like cordwood, to make passage for advancing columns." The Chickamauga lived up to its name that day, he said: "It ran red with blood."

Shortly after 1 p.m. Rosecrans decided

In this unfinished sketch, Confederate troops at Reed's Bridge drive off Colonel Robert Minty's cavalry, shown withdrawing on the far side of the Chickamauga. Minty reported that his men were in the process of demolishing the vital bridge when they were surprised by the Confederate column "moving at the double-quick as steadily as if at drill."

Confederate Brigadier General Bushrod Johnson was chosen to lead the advance across Chickamauga Creek at Reed's Bridge because of his proven reputation for coolness, judgment and daring. He had the capacity in battle, noted a superior, to assess a situation at a glance and to exploit it.

to move his headquarters from Crawfish Springs, southwest of Lee and Gordon's Mill, to be nearer the fighting. He chose the house of a young widow named Eliza Glenn, just behind Thomas' right. Charles A. Dana, a noted journalist who had been appointed Assistant Secretary of War, went with him. "Although closer to the battle," Dana wrote later, "we could see no more of it here than at Crawfish Springs, the conflict being fought altogether in a thick forest, and being invisible to outsiders. The nature of the firing and the reports from the commanders alone enabled us to follow its progress."

Rosecrans tried in vain to find out what was happening — his maps were poor and Thomas was too busy to explain very much, even though they were linked by telegraph. The conflagration was spreading steadily southward and approaching General Rosecrans' headquarters.

Meanwhile Cheatham's troops, who had halted the Union advance near Reed's Bridge, were counterattacked by General Richard Johnson's division. "The line in front of us stalks grimly into the smoke," recalled Sergeant J. K. Young of the 89th Illinois, whose regiment followed in the second wave. "Men cheer, but in that awful roar the voice of a man cannot be heard 10 feet away. Men fall to the right and left. The line stumbles over corpses as it hurries on. There are flashes in the smoke cloud, terrible explosions in the air, and men are stepped on or leaped over as they throw up their arms and fall upon the grass and scream in the agony of mortal wounds." Johnson's attack threatened to pierce the Confederate line, and Bragg sent Major General Alexander P. Stewart's division to Cheatham's support.

As Stewart's men marched up from the south they began to meet wounded Confederates on their way back from the battlefield. One soldier being carried on a litter, his intestines exposed by a terrible wound, waved his hat at the fresh troops and cried, "Boys, when I left we were driving 'em!"

At 2:30 p.m. Stewart came into line on Cheatham's left and plunged into the fight. His assault struck the division of Brigadier General Horatio P. Van Cleve and sent it reeling back past the Brotherton farmhouse. The exchange of gunfire was murderous. One of Stewart's brigades lost 604 men — nearly a third of its strength — in minutes.

Thomas' two other divisions under Reynolds and Negley, hurrying northward to his assistance, were marching past the rear of Van Cleve's division when Stewart attacked. Reynolds immediately joined the fight in support of Van Cleve; Negley stood by in reserve. They were just in time: Stewart had broken the Federal line and had seized the La Fayette road, which linked Thomas' corps with Crittenden's farther to the right, then pushed on to the Glenn-Kelly road. The Confederates now threatened to cut the Dry Valley road, the route between Rosecrans' field headquarters and Chattanooga. The

Federal commander, watching from the Glenn house, was only three quarters of a mile from the action.

Desperately, Van Cleve's troops reformed alongside Reynolds' division in front of the Dry Valley road. There was a momentary respite and then, as Stewart drove forward again, down the blueclad lines came the command "Fire!" Related Captain James Carnahan of the 86th Indiana: "Out from the rifles of the men and the mouths of those cannon leap the death-dealing bullet and canister; again and again, with almost lightning rapidity, they pour in their deadly, merciless fire, until along that entire ridge it had become almost one continuous volley."

General Bragg had been caught off guard by the unexpected beginning of the battle and had not yet ordered a full-scale assault. He was making the mistake of committing his troops piecemeal. D. H. Hill later compared Bragg's tactics that day to "the sparring of the amateur boxer" as opposed to "the crushing blows of the trained pugilist."

All day General Hood had waited for orders, listening impatiently to the sounds of battle around him. At last, shortly after 4 p.m., he took matters into his own hands. He aligned a division under Brigadier General Evander Law beside that of Brigadier General Bushrod Johnson and launched both divisions in an attack against the Federal right. As his fresh troops marched crisply past Stewart's ragged, exhausted soldiers there was an exchange of banter, and a soldier from Hood's Texas Brigade called out a taunt: "Rise up, Tennesseans, and see the Texans go in!"

Hood's attack struck the division of Brigadier General Jefferson C. Davis. In all the shifting of Federal units, Davis' two brigades had been left with both flanks unprotected; and as the Confederates descended on his division with blood-curdling yells, the regiments gave way from left to right. Last to collapse was the brigade commanded by Norwegian-born Colonel Hans Christian Heg. "Bullets tore through the ranks," an Ohio newspaperman recalled; "grape and canister whistled among the brave men who stood their ground, not yielding an inch." Heg was fatally wounded, and 696 of his men were killed, wounded or captured before the embattled brigade fell back. For a moment there seemed to be a real possibility of a Federal rout. Hood's and Johnson's soldiers, fighting their way forward inexorably, approached so close to Rosecrans' headquarters that those inside had to shout to make themselves heard over the roar of battle.

Brigadier General Thomas J. Wood rushed his Federal division into the gap on Davis' right — and now Hood's flank was threatened in its turn. Wilder's Lightning Brigade, deployed on Thomas' right, was in the thick of things as usual. Eli Lilly's artillery galloped forward, set up its guns in a cornfield and let fly at Johnson's left flank. Many of the Confederates had taken shelter in a ditch along the La Fayette road, and the Federal guns enfiladed the position. Within minutes, recalled a gunner, "the ditch was literally full of dead and wounded." The carnage was so great that Wilder quailed. "At this point," he later said, "it actually seemed a pity to kill men so. They fell in heaps, and I had it in my heart to order the firing to cease, to end the awful sight."

By late afternoon every Federal division but two had been engaged in the battle. One was Brigadier General James B. Steedman's

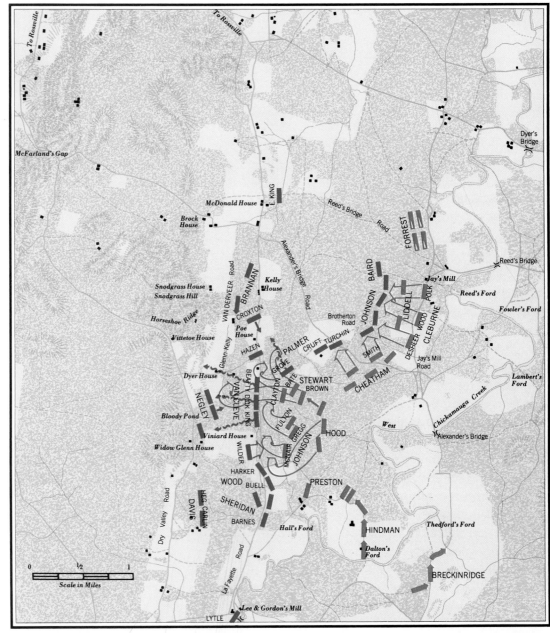

From midafternoon until night on September 19 the two armies surged back and forth, roughly along the lines shown here. Having crossed the meandering Chickamauga, the Confederates launched an attack against Van Cleve's division, bending back the center of the Federal line. Counterattacks by the divisions of Brannan and Negley in the center and Sheridan and Wood on the right halted the Confederates' advance. Cleburne's late-afternoon attack on the Federal left was repulsed by Richard W. Johnson and Absalom Baird.

division of Granger's Reserve Corps, which had been stationed all day far to the north near Rossville, guarding the approaches to Chattanooga. The other, commanded by General Philip Sheridan, now made a timely entry, filing into position next to Wilder to attack. As Sheridan rode up to Wilder, he was preceded by a cluster of pompous staff officers crying out, "Make way for Sheridan! Make way for Sheridan!" Almost immediately, Sheridan launched a fresh assault. Minutes later, repelled in sharp fighting, his men came running back across the road. Whereupon Wilder's troops, in high amuse-ment, called out: "Make way for Sheridan!"

During the fighting Wilder's men captured a teen-age soldier of Hood's command. Up to that time the Federals had not been certain that any of Longstreet's men were on the scene, and Colonel Smith D. Atkins of the 92nd Illinois hurried the prisoner to the commanding general. Rosecrans, who hated to hear bad news — and was especially dreading this particular bad news — was incredulous when the prisoner told him that Longstreet's troops were on the field. He was also furious. He "flew into a passion," said Atkins, and accused the prisoner of lying. The youth was so terrified that he could not utter a sound. Atkins hastily withdrew, taking the prisoner with him. When Rosecrans had cooled down, he was compelled to admit that the soldier had been telling the truth.

It was growing late. The day had been a long, arduous, confused and bloody one for both armies. As the sun set, George Thomas began making new dispositions in preparation for the next morning. Most of his men thought the fighting was finished for a while: Darkness was beginning to fall, and night attacks were rare. But Thomas warned his division commanders to stay alert.

In fact, on the other side of the creek, General Patrick Cleburne's division was toiling northward, having started opposite Lee and Gordon's Mill in midafternoon. As twilight approached, Cleburne's men forded the icy stream in water armpit-deep and, having passed through Walker's lines after sunset, suddenly descended on Thomas.

The day ended as it had begun, in a horrible cacophony. There was "one solid, unbroken wave of awe-inspiring sound," a soldier of the 18th Alabama said. "It seemed as if all the fires of earth and hell had been turned loose in one mighty effort to destroy each other." Cleburne had drilled his men relentlessly, and his division lived up to its reputation as the fastest-firing in Bragg's army.

"Confederate artillery," wrote Federal Captain Ebenezer Wells, "filled the woods with their shells, which in the twilight made the skies seem like a firmament of pestilential stars. The 77th Pennsylvania of the first line was lapped up like a drop of oil under a flame."

Screaming the Rebel yell, Cleburne's men rolled irresistibly forward. In hand-to-hand fighting they took three guns, captured near-

Colonel Hans Christian Heg's 15th Wisconsin faces withering fire from Georgia troops of General Hen

Benning's brigade at Viniard's Farm in the late afternoon of September 19. Heg can be seen falling mortally wounded from his horse at right center.

ly 300 prisoners and gained a mile of ground. They did not stop until it became too dark to see what they were doing. Then at last the firing died away. Cleburne and his soldiers lay down for the night where they were, among the dead and wounded.

It was a night that no one there forgot. The weather had turned bitter cold, and the soldiers of both sides had to sleep on the ground. Most of the troops had no warm clothing or blankets, Cleburne's men were still wet from their immersion in the creek — and all went without fires, which would have made tempting targets. The steady roar of musketry had ended, but no silence descended over the field. "All through the night," recalled a soldier of the 60th Alabama, "a sharp fire was kept up between the pickets, and, ever and anon, the booming of a cannon, startling us in our troubled slumber, reminded of the carnage of the past day and the coming horrors of tomorrow."

What everyone remembered most vividly was the groaning of the wounded. Litter-bearers worked all night, but there were many soldiers they could not reach. "A great many badly wounded men of both armies lay between the lines," recalled a member of Lilly's battery. "The cries and groans from these poor fellows is perfectly awful," he wrote. "They are more dreadful than the storm of bullets that showered on us all day — friend and foe lying side by side, the friends of each unable to assist in the least. It was the hardest part of the battle to lie within hearing and not be able to assist them."

In the woods in front of Cleburne's 6th Texas, a Union officer lay groaning so piteously that the Texans finally could stand it no longer. Risking their own lives, some of them slipped out into the danger zone be-tween the armies and brought the enemy officer back in a blanket. They carried him behind a nearby house and — out of sight of the enemy but in clear violation of orders — they started a small fire to keep him warm.

From every direction could be heard the rumbling of wheels as ambulances picked up the wounded and artillery pieces were moved into position. Both sides were preparing feverishly for the next day's fighting. "The work now begins of throwing up breast-works," wrote one Confederate officer; "at the same time the sound of the ax indicates that the enemy is doing likewise."

The Federal commanders also shifted units around to meet the morning's anticipated assault. There was little sleep for the soldiers. "Much of the night time," a Federal colonel recorded, "was taken up with slow and tiresome marching in the darkness." On top of everything else, the Federals suffered from thirst. The area was still parched by the summerlong drought, and water was scarce. "The Rebels had possession of the Chicka-mauga," a Federal officer said, "and we had to do without."

That night Rosecrans called a council of war at the Glenn house. It had been a rough day; although the Confederates had not broken the Federal line, they had repeatedly come close — and they would be back tomorrow. Too, they were obviously being reinforced and it was assumed that they now outnumbered the Union forces — as indeed they did, about 67,000 to about 57,000. "It struck me that much depression prevailed," Sheridan later recalled. "We were in a bad strait unquestionably."

In the discussion among the Federal commanders it was agreed that the Army of the Cumberland would take a defensive stance

At twilight on September 19, Confederate troops of Patrick Cleburne's division surge forward through the woods to attack the Federal line visible under the trees in the distance. As night fell, troops of both sides had to aim their weapons by sound and muzzle flashes — occasionally firing on their comrades by accident.

on the 20th. Thomas would hold fast where he was, Alexander McCook would close up to his left and Crittenden would stand by in reserve. During the meeting the exhausted General Thomas snoozed in his chair; whenever his opinion was sought he would rouse himself momentarily and say, "I would strengthen the left," and then go back to sleep. Rosecrans agreed to send Negley's division to strengthen Thomas' left flank. The meeting adjourned after midnight.

A Confederate council that night was less formal. Bragg met with Leonidas Polk and some others and announced with no forewarning that he was reorganizing his army yet again. There would now be two wings: The right, consisting of Polk's, Hill's and Walker's corps, was to be commanded by Polk; the left, including Hood, Buckner, and Longstreet's arriving forces, would be led by General Longstreet — who was rumored to be in the area but had not yet made it to headquarters. Hood found little enthusiasm among Bragg's officers for the next

CHICKAMAUGA.

day's work. As he put it: "Not one spoke in a sanguine tone regarding the result of the battle in which we were then engaged."

Longstreet had indeed arrived. He had stepped off his train at the depot in Ringgold at 2 p.m. and had been astonished and exasperated to discover that Bragg had sent no one to brief him — or even to tell him where to find the army's commander.

For two hours Longstreet paced the platform of the little station, until his horse and his staff arrived on another train. Then, accompanied by two aides, he went to look for Bragg, who was a good 20 miles away. The men had no idea where to go; according to Colonel Moxley Sorrel, they "wandered by various roads and across small streams in the growing darkness of the Georgia forest," following the racket of gunfire ahead. They traveled along the narrow roads amid ambulances, stragglers and the walking wounded coming in the opposite direction. At one point they almost blundered into the Federal lines and certain capture. Not until 11 p.m. did Longstreet finally track down Bragg — "about whom by this time," Sorrel later wrote icily, "some hard words were passing." Bragg had gone to bed, but he quickly got up, and for an hour the two men talked.

Bragg's strategy was exactly the same as before: Smash the Federal left and drive Rosecrans into the trap of McLemore's Cove. Polk's right wing would attack at daybreak; Longstreet would then follow suit. The attack was to be in echelon, with the division on the extreme right leading off, and each unit thereafter following the unit on its right into battle.

The orders for the complicated reorganization and attack deployed the corps commanded by D. H. Hill — General John

Breckinridge's and Cleburne's divisions — on Polk's far right. Polk notified the two division commanders of the new plans, which required Breckinridge to march from his position on the left flank all the way to the lead-off position on the extreme right. But Hill never got a copy of the orders. Polk assumed, he later said, that Bragg would pass it along.

The next morning near dawn, about the time the attack should have been starting, Hill finally learned from his division commanders of Bragg's order for the assault. He then decided that his men must eat breakfast before they fought. He notified Polk, saying his forces would not be ready to attack for "an hour or more."

"Hour after hour passed," recalled Confederate Brigadier General Arthur Manigault, whose brigade was in General Longstreet's line near the left flank. "Everything was as quiet as though no human being was within miles, not even a scattering picket shot. Various were the surmises as to the cause of the delay. Had the enemy retreated? Was the order of battle changed? Were we to await the enemy?"

In the meantime, Bragg was fuming as his disbelief mounted. At last he sent a staff officer to find out what was wrong. The officer returned to report that he had found Polk reading a newspaper and waiting for his breakfast. Bragg, according to one account, thereupon "uttered a terrible exclamation, in which Polk, Hill and all his generals were included." Then he personally ordered the battle to begin.

"Just as we began to breathe freely and the intense suspense began to wear off," wrote Manigault, "the report of a distant gun at the extreme right of our line sounded in our ears." More cannon were heard, "and then

Confederate troops of General James Longstreet's I Corps detrain at Ringgold, Georgia, on September 19 on their way to join Bragg's army fighting at Chickamauga Creek. "Never before," recorded a staff officer, "were so many troops moved over such worn-out railways. Never before were such crazy cars — passenger, baggage, mail, coal, box, platform — used for hauling such good soldiers. But we got there nevertheless."

in rapid succession the fire was taken up by half a dozen batteries on either side." Next came the musketry, "gradually growing larger and increasing in volume as the engagement progressed from right to left." The battle was under way — at 9:45 a.m.

Breckinridge's three brigades led the assault on the Federal left; two of them drove around the end of Thomas' position and smashed into Negley's regiments, which were just arriving from farther south. Negley's lead brigade, commanded by Brigadier General John Beatty, was forced back until it was behind the Federal left flank. One of Beatty's regiments, the 88th Indiana, had to change front from north to south as the Confederates stormed in behind it.

One of Breckinridge's brigades was led by

Brigadier General Benjamin Hardin Helm, a brother-in-law of Mary Lincoln, a graduate of West Point and Harvard, and a man much admired by the President. Most of Helm's troops were Kentuckians. While the War lasted, these soldiers could never return to their Union-held state; they were therefore known as the Orphan Brigade.

The Orphans managed to advance to within 30 yards of Thomas' lines, but the fighting was murderous. Private John Green of the 9th Kentucky said that the Orphans were "giving and taking death blows which could last but a few minutes without utter annihilation." Indeed, men were falling all about him, including his regimental and company commanders. General Helm was mortally wounded by a bullet fired from the ranks of the Federal 15th Kentucky.

For a brief moment, Breckinridge's division actually seized the road to Chattanooga, but it could not hold on. Beatty was meanwhile calling desperately for help. The other two brigades of Negley's division never arrived, partly because Negley's replacement in McCook's front line, General Thomas J. Wood's division, had not appeared. When Rosecrans discovered that Wood had failed to march his men forward from their position in reserve, he rushed to confront the division commander and lost his temper. "What is the meaning of this, sir?" Rosecrans shouted. "You have disobeyed my specific orders! By your damnable negligence you are endangering the safety of the entire army, and, by God, I will not tolerate it! Move your division at once, as I have instructed, or the consequences will not be pleasant for yourself!"

Although this blistering public rebuke must have been profoundly resented by Wood, he said nothing and quickly moved his division into position, freeing Negley's remaining troops.

The attack by Breckinridge had been followed by that of the next Confederate division in line, under General Cleburne. As Cleburne's men forged ahead through a pine forest they were suddenly confronted by a line of Federals sheltered behind a formidable log breastwork. The Confederate line was staggered by volleys of musketry and deadly salvos of canister. One of Cleburne's brigade commanders, General James Deshler, was struck in the chest by a shell and his heart was torn from his body. Unable to break the Federal line, the Confederates took shelter behind the trees and blazed away at the defenders.

As Cleburne's assault ground to a stop,

Condemned by some for blindly obeying an order by Rosecrans that opened a massive hole in the Union line, Brigadier General Thomas J. Wood nonetheless was a highly regarded officer whose personal courage was so marked that Sherman once said it was worth 20,000 men.

General Polk committed Walker's and Cheatham's divisions. Once again the Confederate troops charged toward those forbidding log breastworks. Once again they were thrown back with heavy losses.

Thomas' messages asking for reinforcement were practically continuous now, and Rosecrans was pulling units away from the right flank of his line and sending them to Thomas as fast as he could free them.

Then, about 10:30 a.m., one of Thomas' staff officers, Captain Sanford Kellogg, returned from Rosecrans' headquarters with alarming news: Passing along the Federal

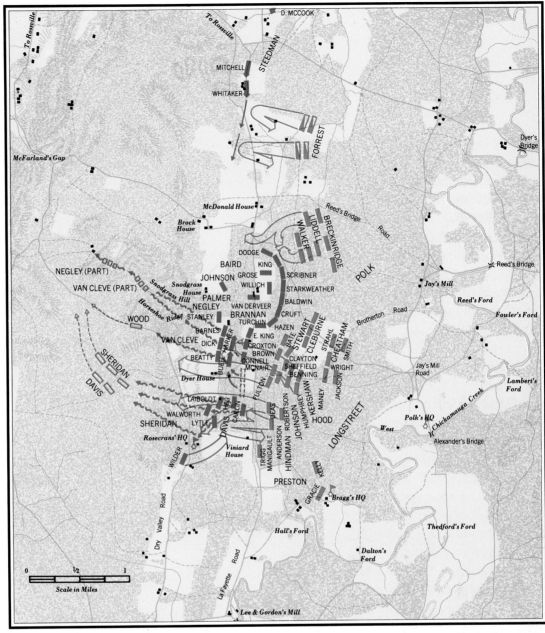

Map labels (as they appear on the map):

To Rossville · D. MCCOOK · MITCHELL · STEEDMAN · WHITAKER · FORREST · Dyer's Bridge · McFarland's Gap · McDonald House · Reed's Bridge Road · LIDDELL · WALKER · BRECKINRIDGE · Brock House · DODGE · BAIRD · KING · POLK · Reed's Bridge · JOHNSON · GROSE · SCRIBNER · Jay's Mill · NEGLEY (PART) · WILLICH · STARKWEATHER · Reed's Ford · VAN CLEVE (PART) · Snodgrass Hill · PALMER · VAN DERVEER · BALDWIN · Fowler's Ford · Snodgrass House · NEGLEY · BRANNAN · CRUFT · Horseshoe Ridge · STANLEY · TURCHIN · HAZEN · STEWART · Brotherton Road · WOOD · BARNES · E. KING · BATE · CLEBURNE · Jay's Mill Road · VAN CLEVE · DICK · CROXTON · STRAHL · BROWN · CLAYTON · CHEATHAM · Lambert's Ford · BEATTY · O'CONNELL · SHEFFIELD · WRIGHT · SMITH · McNAIR · BENNING · JACKSON · SHERIDAN · Dyer House · BUELL · HARKER · MANEY · DAVIS · FULTON · KERSHAW · Polk's HQ · LAIBOLDT · HEG · HUMPHREY · West · Alexander's Bridge · WALWORTH · CARLIN · JOHNSON · HOOD · SHERIDAN · LYTLE · DEAS · ROBERTSON · Rosecrans' HQ · ANDERSON · LONGSTREET · WILDER · Viniard House · TRIGG · HINDMAN · MANIGAULT · GRACIE · KELLY · PRESTON · Bragg's HQ · Dry Valley Road · Hall's Ford · Thedford's Ford · La Fayette Road · Dalton's Ford · Lee & Gordon's Mill

0 · ½ · 1
Scale in Miles

When General Wood shifted his division to the left at Chickamauga on the morning of September 20, he set in motion a critical sequence of attacks. Longstreet immediately drove into the gap in the Union line with five divisions, led by Bushrod Johnson. Hindman routed Sheridan and Davis, and Hood veered to the right to overrun Brannan in the woods. Wilder's counterattack slowed but did not halt the onrushing Confederates.

lines, he had noted a gap near the center, presumably at a point where a division had been pulled out to help Thomas. Whatever the reason, there was a hole, he told Thomas, between the division of General Wood and the division to the north under Reynolds. Thomas immediately notified Rosecrans — and Rosecrans reacted instantly with an urgent message to Wood: "The general commanding directs that you close up on Reynolds as fast as possible, and support him."

Wood was puzzled. He knew that there was no gap: The division of General Brannan was between Wood and Reynolds, although drawn back into the forest, where it apparently had been invisible to Captain Kellogg. Nevertheless, Wood was reluctant to invite another dressing down for not obeying Rosecrans' commands. He began to move his division behind Brannan to join Reynolds.

Around 11:30 a.m. Rosecrans ordered Davis forward from his position in reserve to the south to take Wood's place. At the same time two of Sheridan's brigades, in the line to the right of Wood, were sent north to support Thomas. Now two Federal divisions and part of a third were in sidelong motion, and there was a quarter-mile gap in the cen-

ter of the line where Wood had been. At that moment, entirely by chance, James Longstreet unleashed three divisions — Hood's and Johnson's abreast, Brigadier General Joseph B. Kershaw's behind — directly into the Federal gap. As the juggernaut of 23,000 troops stormed across the La Fayette road and through the fields of the Brotherton farm, stark panic struck the Federal right.

Bushrod Johnson, in the vanguard of the Confederate attack, later issued an official report that fairly glowed with exultation: "The scene now presented was unspeakably grand. The resolute and impetuous charge, the rush of our heavy columns sweeping out from the shadow and gloom of the forest and into the open fields flooded with sunlight, the glitter of arms, the onward dash of artillery and mounted men, the retreat of the foe, the shouts of the hosts of our army, the dust, the smoke, the noise of firearms — of whistling balls and grapeshot and of bursting shell — made up a battle scene of unsurpassed grandeur." Despite heavy losses, Johnson's right-flank brigade under General Evander McNair surged toward two batteries of Federal artillery. The gunners fired round after round into the gray tide and, as the Confederates swarmed over their cannon, fought hand to hand. In desperation some artillerymen hurled grapeshot and shells with their bare hands.

Just as Johnson's men paused in a clearing near the Dyer farm to catch their breath, Hood rode up, his left arm still in a sling from the wounding at Gettysburg. "Go ahead," he ordered Johnson, "and keep ahead of everything." Johnson got his troops to their feet once again. "With a shout along my entire front," Hood recorded, "the Confederates rushed forward, penetrated into

The name "Chickamauga" is prominently displayed on a battle flag of the — Arkansas, a regiment that played — vital role in Cleburne's assaults — the Federal left early on the second day of the battle. The crossed — cannon at the flag's center signify that — regiment had captured enemy artillery in one or more of their many — battles, as they did at Chickamauga.

Confederate troops load and fire their rifles in the tangled woodland along Chickamauga Creek. The heavily thicketed terrain, noted a Union officer, made for a "mad, irregular battle, very much resembling guerrilla warfare on a vast scale, in which one army was bushwhacking the other."

the woods, over and beyond the enemy's breastworks, and thus achieved another glorious victory for our arms.''

Suddenly a brigade of Federals counterattacked, and Hood himself was shot — "pierced,'' he wrote, "with a Minié ball in the upper third of the right leg.'' He toppled off his horse and was caught by Texans of his old brigade. As Confederate reserves came into action, Hood was tenderly borne to the rear, where the broken leg was amputated.

On Hood's left, Major General Thomas C. Hindman's division was likewise gaining ground. In minutes the first Federal line, Jefferson Davis' division, was shattered and fleeing in panic. The fugitives plowed into the ranks of the second line, Sheridan's division, throwing those troops into disorder. Soon the better part of McCook's corps was streaming rearward, toward Rosecrans' headquarters at the Glenn house.

The only one of McCook's units to offer resistance was a brigade commanded by Brigadier General William H. Lytle, a popular author and poet who had become a hard-fighting and capable commander. Lytle halted on a hill just north of the Glenn house, telling his officers that the brigade "would die in their tracks, with their harness on.'' Then, as Hindman's Confederates surged toward the front and both flanks, Lytle decided on a desperate stratagem. Spurring his horse to the front of the Federal line, he shouted to his outnumbered command, "All right, men, we can die but once. This is the time and place. Let us charge.''

The hopeless attack was shattered almost immediately. Lytle was shot in the spine but continued to ride among his men until three more bullets knocked him to the ground. With their commander dying, the survivors joined the stampede for the rear.

At Rosecrans' headquarters, Charles Dana, who had been awake for much of the previous two nights, had stretched out on the grass and gone to sleep. At the onset of Longstreet's attack, Dana recalled, "I was awakened by the most infernal noise I ever heard.

With his arm in a sling from his Gettysburg wound, Major General John Hood reels in the saddle as he is struck by a Minié ball while rallying his Texas troops at Chickamauga. Noting that the general was wounded both at Gettysburg and at Chickamauga while riding unfamiliar horses, Hood's omen-conscious Texans concluded he was safe only when on the back of his favorite roan, Jeff Davis.

I sat up on the grass, and the first thing I saw was General Rosecrans crossing himself — he was a very devout Catholic. 'Hello!' I said to myself, 'if the general is crossing himself, we are in a desperate situation.' "

Dana leaped on his horse. "I had no sooner collected my thoughts and looked around toward the front, where all this din came from, than I saw our lines break and melt away like leaves before the wind." Rosecrans' calm voice rose above the hubbub. "If you care to live any longer," he told his staff, "get away from here." Dana wrote: "Then the headquarters around me disappeared. The graybacks came through with a rush, and soon the musket balls and the cannon shot began to reach the place where he stood. The whole right of the army had apparently been routed."

A mile or so to the northeast, Longstreet was jubilant. "They have fought their last man," an artilleryman heard him say, "and *he* is running." Bragg's instructions had been to exert pressure on the left, to drive Rosecrans' army toward McLemore's Cove. But except for Wilder's brigade, which was harassing the flank of Hindman's division, the Federal right had disintegrated. Bushrod Johnson had begun to wheel toward his right, and Longstreet urged him on. If he could destroy Thomas, Rosecrans' entire army would be a shambles.

The Federals had been fighting with their backs to Missionary Ridge; with heavy fighting continuing across the Rossville road to the north, the only avenue of retreat left to the soldiers fleeing before Longstreet was McFarland's Gap, leading through the ridge to the west. Toward this narrow opening now poured the disorganized units from the army's shattered right wing — the better part of five Federal divisions. A reporter from the Cincinnati *Gazette* watched from the crest of the ridge: "Men, animals, vehicles, became a mass of struggling, cursing, shouting, frightened life. Everything and everybody appeared to dash headlong for the narrow gap, and men, horses, mules, ambulances, baggage wagons, ammunition wagons, artillery carriages and caissons were rolled and tumbled together in a confused, inextricable, and finally motionless mass, completely blocking up the mouth of the gap."

Lieutenant Colonel Gates Thruston, an officer on McCook's staff, saw Rosecrans trying to reach Sheridan for help; the commander was repulsed by "a storm of canister and musketry," Thruston recalled. "All became confusion. No order could be heard above the tempest of battle. With a wild yell the Confederates swept on far to their left. They seemed everywhere victorious. Rosecrans was borne back in the retreat." At the mouth of McFarland's Gap, Rosecrans and his chief of staff, Brigadier General James A. Garfield, tried to take a side road back toward the left wing and George Thomas, but enemy forces blocked their way; instead they pushed on through the gap five miles farther to Rossville. There, amid what an eyewitness described as "driving masses of teamsters, stragglers and fugitives," the two men paused to consider — and to rest their horses, blown by the swift ride.

There was another crossroad at Rossville, and therefore another opportunity to join Thomas. But the sounds of battle were now barely audible; was he still fighting? Rosecrans and Garfield dismounted and put their ears to the ground. They could hear little except occasional distant musketry. They sought information from some disheveled

The Fallen Commanders

The fighting at Chickamauga claimed 35,000 casualties, more than any other battle in the Civil War's Western Theater. "The losses are heavy on both sides," reported Confederate commander Braxton Bragg, "especially so in officers." Indeed, during the confused fighting in the heavily wooded terrain many senior officers were cut down — including the eight gallant brigade commanders shown here.

General James Deshler, a West Pointer and veteran of the Indian Wars, was killed by a shell while personally inspecting his men's frontline ammunition supply prior to ordering an attack. General Preston Smith and Colonel Philemon Baldwin were hit almost simultaneously at twilight on September 19: Baldwin was riddled with bullets while attempting to rally the men of his old regiment, and Smith was shot when he led his troops into the Federal lines.

Most of the officers who saw death coming faced it with soldierly aplomb. As thousands of Confederates swept toward his beleaguered brigade, General William Lytle, a poet and author, announced calmly to his staff, "If I must die, I will die as a gentleman." Some found strength in their convictions and in the justness of their cause. As he lay dying, Mary Lincoln's brother-in-law, Confederate General Benjamin Hardin Helm, uttered over and over again the single word "victory."

BRIGADIER GENERAL
JAMES DESHLER, C.S.A.
Killed September 20

BRIGADIER GENERAL
PRESTON SMITH, C.S.A.
**Mortally wounded
September 19**

BRIGADIER GENERAL
BENJAMIN HARDIN HELM, C.S.A.
**Mortally wounded
September 20**

COLONEL PEYTON H.
COLQUITT, C.S.A.
**Mortally wounded
September 20**

BRIGADIER GENERAL
WILLIAM H. LYTLE, U.S.A.
Killed September 20

COLONEL EDWARD A. KING,
U.S.A.
Killed September 20

COLONEL HANS CHRISTIAN
HEG, U.S.A.
Mortally wounded
September 19

COLONEL PHILEMON P.
BALDWIN, U.S.A.
Killed September 19

soldiers around them — and were told that "the entire army was defeated and in retreat to Chattanooga." The same soldiers said they were from Negley's division; that unit, they declared, had been "knocked all to pieces." Here was dismaying news. When Rosecrans had last seen Negley, the division commander was on his way to join Thomas with two brigades; if Negley's command was shattered, the entire left wing was doubtless defeated and in disarray.

Rosecrans was upset and distracted. Nevertheless, he was determined to try to join Thomas and save what he could of the wrecked army. He ordered Garfield to proceed to Chattanooga and prepare the defenses there. The Confederates were sure to attack the town and much needed to be done; he issued a long list of instructions.

At that, Garfield demurred. Rosecrans, he said, must go to Chattanooga himself to lay out a new defensive line and position the returning units along it. The orders would be complicated, and Rosecrans could spell them out more effectively than anyone else. "I can go to General Thomas and report the situation to you," Garfield said, "much better than I can give those orders." Rosecrans agreed and made his way north.

Rosecrans, severely shaken, arrived at the headquarters building in Chattanooga at 4 p.m. He was by then unable to dismount or to walk unassisted. His aides helped the distraught general into the house. Once inside, Rosecrans slumped in a chair, his head in his hands, the picture of despair.

Charles Dana arrived in Chattanooga soon afterward and sent a grim telegram to Washington. "My report today is of deplorable importance," it began. "Chickamauga is as fatal a day in our history as Bull Run."

The battle was, in fact, far from over. George Thomas, still only vaguely aware of what had occurred to the rest of Rosecrans' army, was engaged in the fight of his life.

The right of this line, Brannan's division and part of Wood's, faced south from the crest of an elevation that projected from Missionary Ridge. A part of this rise was known as Snodgrass Hill, after a family that lived nearby; the whole of the eminence may not have had a name, but it quickly acquired one — Horseshoe Ridge. The main line, held by Baird's, Johnson's, Reynolds' and Major General John Palmer's divisions, faced east from their original positions near the La Fayette road. To the rear of the position were the roads leading west to McFarland's Gap, and north to Rossville and Chattanooga.

As a result of Thomas' repeated calls for reinforcements, he now had under him units from three of Rosecrans' corps — perhaps half of the Army of the Cumberland. And he was also collecting a ragtag-and-bobtail assortment of units from company to brigade strength, plus a number of soldiers of all ranks who had become separated from the rest of the army during the hard fighting on the right. Many officers were behind the breastworks fighting as enlisted men.

The stolid Thomas was not given to dramatics, but as he rode along the lines his very presence bolstered the morale of his battered, powder-stained soldiers. When he came to Colonel Charles Harker's brigade on the left flank he told its commander, "This hill must be held and I trust you to do it." The scrappy Harker replied, "We will hold it or die here."

Among all his other worries, Thomas was concerned about the location of Sheridan's division. He had asked that morning to have

Sheridan sent up from the Federal right but had heard nothing since. At last, around 2 p.m. he sent a messenger to find out what was wrong. The courier quickly returned to report that a large force was approaching from the right rear, behind Reynolds.

From the crest of Snodgrass Hill, Thomas peered out over the field. He could see troops coming through the dust — and they were wearing blue. Could that be Sheridan at last? But Thomas was a careful man, and there had been reports that some Confederates in this battle had blue uniforms. He instructed an officer nearby to have his men wave Union flags. The flags quickly drew fire. These were hostile forces — Longstreet's men, and they were renewing the attack.

Thomas ordered a brigade under Brigadier General William B. Hazen into the line on Snodgrass Hill. The new arrivals were scarcely in position behind some low breastworks, recalled Lieutenant Colonel Robert L. Kimberly of the 41st Ohio, "when the Confederate storm burst. The slope in front of the brigade was open ground, and in a moment this was covered with heavy masses of the enemy making for the top. Hazen's regiments were lying flat. The foremost sprang to its feet, delivered its volley and went down again to load, and the next regiment just behind rose to fire and fall flat while the third put in its work, and so on."

The attacking Confederates, several brigades under the overall direction of General Kershaw, pushed to within 40 paces of the Federal line. There they met such heavy and sustained fire that Kershaw ordered them back. "The slope," said Kimberly, "was strewn with Confederate dead and wounded, but not a man could reach the crest."

Kershaw struck again and again, one fero-

The Legendary Johnny Clem

"He was an expert drummer," wrote his sister, "and being a bright, cheery child, soon made his way into the affections of officers and soldiers." He made his way, also, into the hearts of Northerners, who found the "Drummer Boy of Chickamauga" a most appealing war hero.

Ohio-born Johnny Clem ran away to war before he was 10. He was with the 22nd Michigan in its major battles — Shiloh, Perryville, Murfreesboro, Atlanta — but became famous only after the press extolled his exploits at Chickamauga. Armed with a sawed-off musket cut down to fit him, he shot and wounded a Confederate officer who was said to have galloped upon him shouting, "Surrender, you little Yankee devil!" Other stories had him firing furiously after his drum was ripped away by a shell. He was given a sergeant's stripes for valor and awarded a silver medal by the beautiful daughter of Treasury Secretary Salmon Chase.

The War shaped his life: Appointed a second lieutenant in the postwar Army, he served until 1915. When he retired at 65 he was Major General John L. Clem, the last man active in the armed forces who had fought in the Civil War.

JOHNNY CLEM

cious assault after another. He finally stopped because his troops were out of breath; Colonel William Oates of the 15th Alabama said his men were "panting like dogs tired out in the chase."

Next Bushrod Johnson's and Thomas Hindman's divisions launched another series of charges, aimed like a battering-ram at Thomas' right and rear. It was evident to Thomas that the crisis was at hand; if he could not push Johnson and Hindman back, his escape route would soon be cut off. Worse, his soldiers were running out of ammunition. The men on Horseshoe Ridge were desperately snatching cartridges from the dead and wounded. For a time it looked as if the Federal line would break. "Our troops were driven from the crest, and the enemy's flag waved above it," General John Beatty recalled. Beatty rallied his brigade and led it back up the hill, "waving my hat

and shouting like a madman." The crest was retaken, but Thomas and his troops were in dire straits and there was no solution in sight. Then, suddenly, help was at hand.

All during the fighting of the 19th and for most of the morning of the 20th, Major General Gordon Granger and his Reserve Corps — consisting in its entirety of three inexperienced brigades — had stood guard with increasing impatience over the Rossville road three miles north of the fighting, as ordered by Rosecrans.

At 11 a.m. on the 20th, while Polk's divisions marched to attack Thomas, Granger — a short, pugnacious West Pointer — watched the dust rising in the distance and growled to Major Joseph S. Fullerton, his chief of staff: "They are concentrating over there. That's where we ought to be." As the sounds of battle came rumbling over the fields and more dust and battle smoke rose into the air,

Granger almost exploded with pent-up frustration. "Why the hell does Rosecrans keep me here?" he cried out to Fullerton. "There is the battle!" He climbed up on a haystack and stared into the distance through his field glasses, and at last he could stand it no longer. He uttered an oath and declared: "I am going to Thomas, orders or no orders!"

He commanded Colonel Dan McCook to guard the road with his brigade and within minutes was marching off to join Thomas with the remainder of his corps: a single division under General Steedman.

At Snodgrass Hill, with Hindman, Johnson and Kershaw pounding him from the south, General Thomas stared through his field glasses at the enormous column of dust approaching from the north. Once again he and his officers wondered who was coming — "agitated," as General Beatty put it, "by doubt and hope." Were these their saviors or more enemies? The usually imperturbable Thomas was so jumpy that his horse began fidgeting, making it impossible for him to use his field glasses. Someone said he thought he could see a Union flag. "Do you think so? Do you think so?" asked Thomas anxiously. A few minutes later Granger and Steedman were on the scene, and the defenders felt, in Beatty's words, "a throb of exultation." The newcomers had brought not only fresh soldiers but also fresh supplies of ammunition.

The burly Steedman galloped into action at the head of his division. When the 115th Illinois wavered in the face of Confederate fire, Steedman snatched up its flag and turned to face the enemy alone. "Go back, boys, go back," he roared, "but the flag can't go with you!" The men rallied and charged once again. Steedman's horse was shot out

from under him, and the general was badly bruised by the fall, but he continued to lead his men on foot, flag in hand.

Steedman's troops extended the line on Brannan's right, where Hindman's Confederates were threatening to flank the Federals. In the 20 minutes that followed, Steedman's green soldiers smashed Hindman's attack — but at a terrible cost. Of Steedman's 3,500 Federals, 20 per cent were killed or wounded in those few minutes; among the casualties were six regimental commanders.

By now all of Thomas' units had taken

Covering the Union withdrawal toward Chattanooga, troops of Brigadier General Absalom Baird's division stand fast before the Kelly house in the late afternoon of September 20. "We held our position, yielding not an inch," wrote Baird. "To fall back was more difficult than to remain."

heavy casualties. The total number of men who served under him during the day has been estimated at 25,000; by one account only a quarter of these troops were still in action when Granger showed up. Since that morning, Thomas had fought virtually every brigade in Bragg's army, and toward the end he was fighting them all — Polk's troops as well as Longstreet's.

And still Thomas held. As the shadows deepened, Longstreet redoubled his efforts. He committed his single remaining division, Brigadier General William Preston's, and by early evening he was hitting the Federal line at every point. By Longstreet's own estimate he sent a total of 25 attacks against the Federals. One of the last, and perhaps the fiercest, was the charge of a newly enlisted brigade led by Brigadier General Archibald Gracie Jr. Leaping over the bodies of the dead and dying from earlier assaults, Gracie's troops clawed their way to within feet of the Federal breastworks. In places, the opposing soldiers grappled hand to hand before Gracie's decimated regiments fell back. In the charge, the 1st Alabama Battalion lost nearly 65 per cent of its men, while the flag of the 2nd Battalion was pierced by 83 bullets.

Around 4 p.m. James Garfield showed up, having made a perilous trip down the Rossville road accompanied by two orderlies and a captain acting as guide. They had come under sharp fire; both of the orderlies had been killed and the captain injured. Garfield's horse, badly hurt, managed to get him to Thomas before it collapsed.

At last Thomas learned what had happened to the rest of Rosecrans' army and received instructions from Rosecrans to withdraw from the field immediately. That was manifestly impossible. "It will ruin the army to withdraw it now," Thomas told Garfield. "This position must be held until night."

Garfield accordingly dispatched a message informing Rosecrans in Chattanooga that Thomas was fighting off the Confederates and was "standing like a rock." Reprinted in newspapers all over the country, the message made a hero of the doughty XIV Corps commander, who would be known for the rest of his life as the "Rock of Chickamauga."

As twilight descended over the battlefield, Thomas went to work to get his men safely away. The Confederate attacks were continuing with undiminished intensity, and Thomas was once again running low on ammunition as he began his withdrawal. His plan was to withdraw his divisions in sequence, starting with the southernmost, under Reynolds. Each division was to march behind those still in line toward the safety of McFarland's Gap. But at 5:30 p.m., as Reynolds was leaving, St. John Liddell's Confederates suddenly launched a savage blow straight toward him, endangering the entire Federal position. General Thomas, who was on the scene, commandeered the

Brigadier General Frank C. Armstrong's cavalry helped repulse the assault on the Confederate right during the first day at Chickamauga. On the second day, Armstrong's troopers, fighting dismounted, were praised by General D. H. Hill for "moving like veteran infantry." Born in Arkansas, educated in Massachusetts, Armstrong began the War fighting on the Union side at the Battle of Bull Run. But three weeks later he resigned to join the Confederate Army.

brigade led by General John Turchin and wheeled the troops around. Gesturing toward the oncoming Confederates, Thomas said, "There they are. Clear them out." Turchin launched a furious attack and sent the Confederates reeling back. In the process his men captured 200 prisoners. Then Turchin rejoined Reynolds' retreating division.

One by one, the hard-pressed units left the field and hurried toward safety. In the end only three regiments remained on Snodgrass Hill: the 21st and 89th Ohio and the 22nd Michigan. They were still fighting off attacks, and as the rest of the Federals began their movement toward McFarland's Gap the three regiments were threatened anew. Brannan hurried to Granger, who had been left in command of the field while Thomas supervised the withdrawal, and cried: "The enemy are forming for another assault; we have not another round of ammunition —

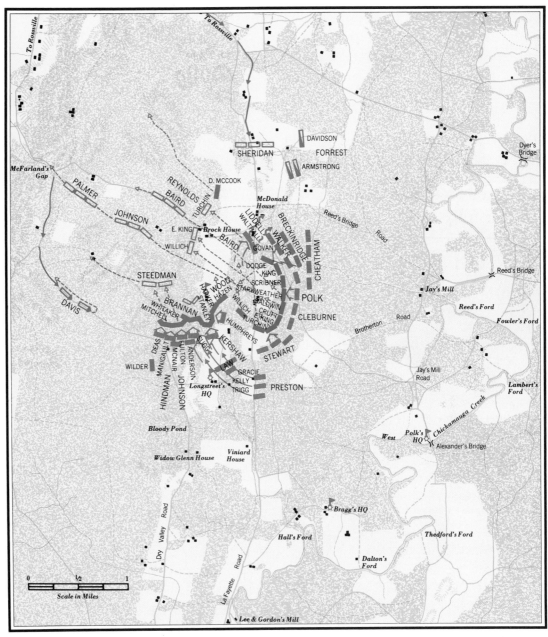

After the Federal center collapsed, General George Thomas formed a south-facing defensive line on Snodgrass Hill and along adjacent high ground known as Horseshoe Ridge. Against this line General James Longstreet threw four divisions — Kershaw's, Hindman's, Bushrod Johnson's and finally Preston's. All afternoon the troops defending the ridge, and those still holding out on the Federal left, repulsed attack after attack. Critical in checking Bushrod Johnson's many assaults was the arrival of Steedman's reserve division on Brannan's right flank.

what shall we do?" Granger said, "Fix bayonets and go for them."

Granger's staff officer, Major Fullerton, recalled: "Along the whole line ran the order, 'Fix bayonets.' On came the enemy — our men were lying down. 'Forward,' was sounded. In one instant they were on their feet. Forward they went to meet the charge. So impetuous was this counter-charge that one regiment, with empty muskets and empty cartridge-boxes, broke through the enemy's line, which, closing in their rear, carried them off as in the undertow." Brannan's charge was gallant but ineffective. There was

little the Federals could do without ammunition, and within minutes the bloodied defenders were surrounded and overwhelmed by General Preston's Confederates. In the three regiments, 322 soldiers were killed or wounded and 563 captured. Only one of the six regimental flags was saved.

The last Federal survivors slipped away after darkness had fallen, when the Confederate fire was diminishing. Without light, Bragg's troops were beginning to fire into one another from the opposite sides of the salient. It had been a brilliant withdrawal under the nose of the enemy. "Like magic,"

A firm believer that success on the battlefield was largely "a question of nerve," the Union's Major General George Thomas set up his command post in a clump of dead trees 400 yards from the fighting on Snodgrass Hill. From there he ranged the front lines urging his weary troops to stand fast.

As troops in the rear pass up newly loaded rifles, Federals on Snodgrass Hill blaze away at attacking Confederates at the end of the da

Two brigades of General Gordon Granger's Reserve Corps sustained 44 per cent casualties in less than two hours when Granger went to aid Thomas on Horseshoe Ridge. From 1 p.m. to dusk, he recalled, "our whole line was continually enveloped in smoke and fire."

on September 20. A Union officer noted that the defenders "fought with the desperation of men standing in their last stronghold."

71

The Snodgrass house on the battle field of Chickamauga. near here Genl Thomas repulsed the last charge made by the confederate army. — It was once said by a Confed. General, that "Here, at Snodgrass house, fell the southern Confederacy"

Longstreet wrote later, "the Union army had melted away in our presence."

The Federal escape chafed Longstreet, but his troops were only too pleased to discover that their enemy had retreated. When the Confederates realized what had happened, they produced a loud and prolonged din of Rebel yells to celebrate their victory. The sound seemed to envelop the fleeing Federals, said Lieutenant Ambrose Bierce of William Hazen's brigade. "It was the ugliest sound that any mortal ever heard," he wrote, "even a mortal exhausted and unnerved by two days of hard fighting, without sleep, without rest, without food, and without hope. There was, however, a space somewhere at the back of us across which that horrible yell did not prolong itself — and through that we finally retired in profound silence and dejection, unmolested."

For the soldiers in blue, the march to Rossville was grim. Beatty recalled, "All along the road, for miles, wounded men were lying. They had crawled or hobbled slowly away from the fury of the battle, become exhausted, and lay down by the roadside to die. Some were calling the names and numbers of their regiments, but many had become too weak to do this; by midnight the column had passed by. What must have been their agony, mental and physical, as they lay in the dreary woods, sensible that there was no one to comfort or to care for them, and that in a few hours more their career on earth would be ended."

General Thomas collected his battered forces at Rossville and formed new lines in expectation of further fighting. The Confederates, as well, made preparations for more action. "I ordered my line to remain as it was," recalled General Longstreet, "am-

munition boxes to be filled, stragglers to be collected, and everything in readiness for the pursuit in the morning."

Polk got Bragg out of bed to report that the Federal army was in full flight and could be destroyed before Rosecrans had a chance to throw up adequate defenses. But Bragg, said an aide who was present, "could not be induced to look at it in that light, and refused to believe that we had won a victory."

Bragg's generals produced a Confederate soldier who had been captured and then had escaped. He had seen the Federal disarray for himself and was brought before Bragg to testify that the enemy was indeed in full retreat. Bragg would not accept the man's story. "Do you know what a retreat looks like?" he asked, acidly. The soldier stared back and said: "I ought to, General; I've been with you during your whole campaign."

Bragg had his reasons for not wanting to

On the north slope of Snodgrass Hill, the log-and-clay Snodgrass house and the field before it marked the last point of desperate Union resistance before Thomas withdrew through McFarland's Gap to Chattanooga. The scrawled commentary is probably by the sketch's unknown artist.

continue the fight. His men were exhausted. Losses on both sides had been enormous, and although no one yet knew the totals, Confederate casualties had been greater than those suffered by the Federals: The Confederates had lost 18,454 killed, wounded or captured, including nine brigade and two division commanders; Federal losses numbered 16,179, including seven brigade commanders. These had been the bloodiest two days of the War.

The Confederate losses in draft animals had been, from a military point of view, every bit as devastating. General Bragg estimated that he had lost about one third of his artillery horses. When someone pressed him to pursue Thomas he replied testily: "How can I? Here is two fifths of my army left on the field, and my artillery is without horses." His wagon trains did not have suffi-

cient horses, either, and supplies were short.

None of this made any sense to Nathan Bedford Forrest. He confronted Bragg on the night of September 21 and urged an advance northward; it was still not too late. "We can get all the supplies our army needs in Chattanooga," he argued. When Bragg was adamant, Forrest could scarcely contain his fury. "What does he fight battles for?" he later snarled to his officers.

By September 22, the entire Federal army was safely within the Chattanooga defenses, and those works were being improved hourly. Bragg moved to the outskirts of the town. He had an idea: If he could occupy Missionary Ridge to the east and Lookout Mountain to the west, he could starve Rosecrans into submission. "We held him at our mercy," he would later say, "and his destruction was only a question of time."

The Awesome Repeating Rifles

Most Civil War soldiers on both sides fought from beginning to end with muzzle-loading rifles. But in 1863 several units of the Federal Army of the Cumberland received a supply of revolutionary weapons. The firearms were multishot repeating rifles developed by two ingenious New England gunsmiths, Samuel Colt and Christopher Spencer.

The new weapons immediately proved their value. At the Battle of Chickamauga, two Federal units used their repeaters to devastating effect, helping to prevent a complete Federal rout. In five hours of fighting, the 535 men of the 21st Ohio fired an astonishing 43,550 rounds with their Colt revolving rifles. "My God," said a dazed Confederate prisoner, "we thought you had a division here."

At the same time, Colonel John T. Wilder's mounted infantry brigade broke up a powerful Confederate attack with their Spencer repeaters. "The effect was awful," Wilder reported. "The head of the attacking column seemed to melt away or sink into the earth."

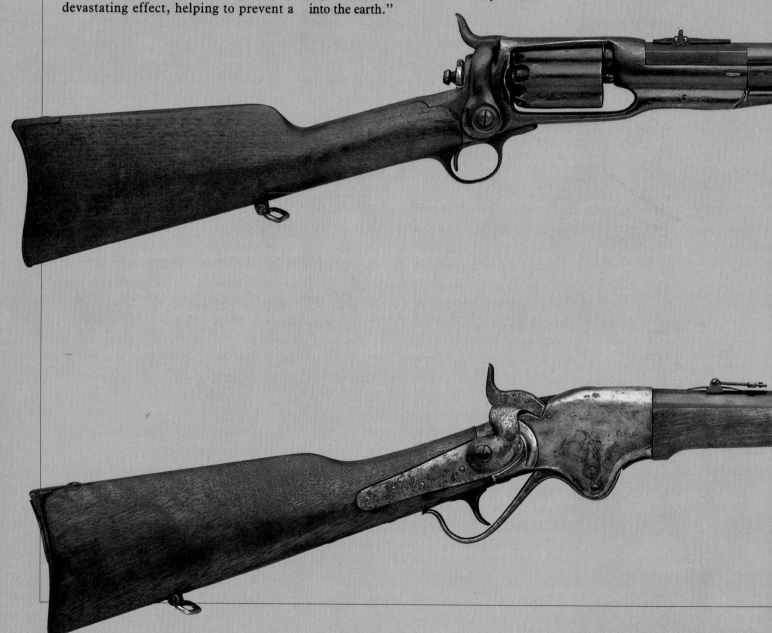

Grouped with one of their officers, five men of the 21st Ohio hold their carefully burnished .56-caliber Colt revolving rifles. To make the new weapon (*below*), Samuel Colt took the revolving action that he used in his famous pistols and adapted it to a long-barreled rifle with a full stock.

A foot soldier turned horseman, Private John M. Munson of Wilder's mounted brigade retains an infantryman's standard outfit — but also carries a Spencer repeater. Most of Wilder's men possessed the full-length, 47-inch rifle shown below, but some carried the shorter 39-inch Spencer carbine, which was better suited to use on horseback.

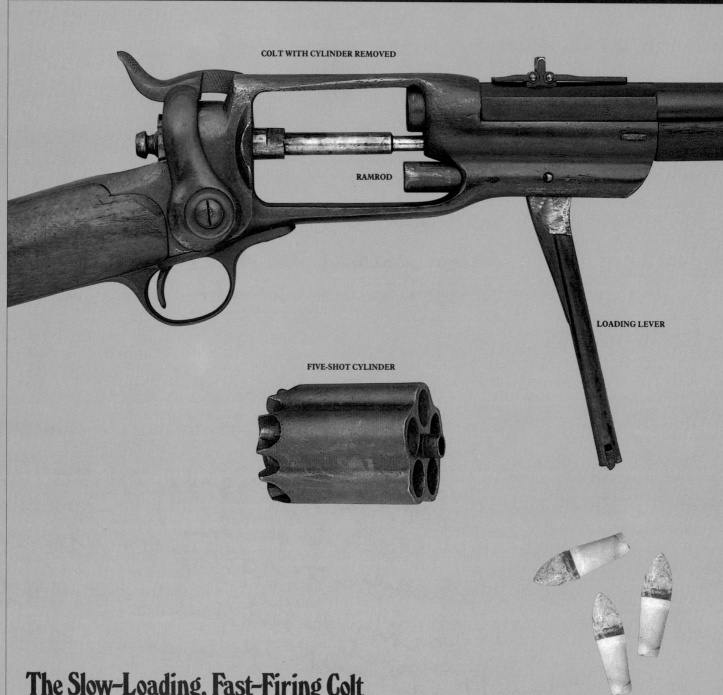

COLT WITH CYLINDER REMOVED

RAMROD

LOADING LEVER

FIVE-SHOT CYLINDER

COLT CARTRIDGES

The Slow-Loading, Fast-Firing Colt

To load the .56-caliber Colt revolving rifle, a soldier first half-cocked the hammer, allowing the cylinder to rotate freely. He then pushed a paper or parchment cartridge, with bullet attached, into one of the cylinder's five chambers. Next he turned the cylinder so that the loaded chamber was in the bottom position, and finally he pulled the lever activating the ramrod, which firmly seated the bullet.

After repeating this process four times more, the soldier placed percussion caps on the nipples that fired each of the chambers. Once he had loaded the weapon, a rifleman could fire the five rounds as swiftly as he was able to cock the hammer and pull the trigger — about nine seconds in all.

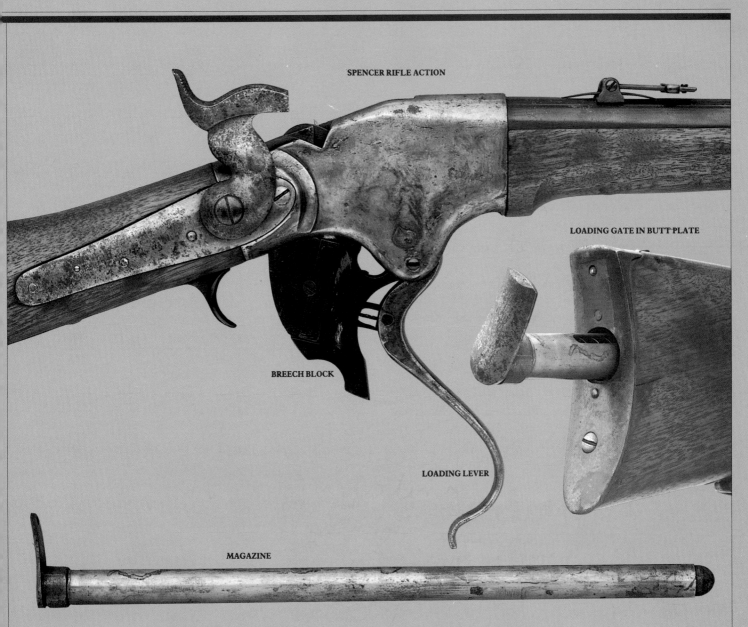

SPENCER RIFLE ACTION

LOADING GATE IN BUTT PLATE

BREECH BLOCK

LOADING LEVER

MAGAZINE

COPPER RIM-FIRE CARTRIDGES

The Rugged, Lever-Action Spencer

Key to the operation of the Spencer rifle was a recently developed copper cartridge that combined primer, powder and bullet in one case. The rifle's hammer detonated mercury fulminate in the cartridge rim. This ignited the powder and discharged the round.

Seven cartridges fitted into a tubelike magazine, which was inserted through the butt. To put a round in the breech for firing, a soldier depressed the loading lever, pulling down the breech block. A spring in the magazine then fed a round into the mechanism. When the soldier raised the lever, the breech block seated the round in the firing chamber. The mechanism also extracted an empty case each time it was loaded.

Besieged Chattanooga

"Two weeks ago this army, elated by a great victory, was in readiness to pursue its defeated enemy. Today, it is certain that the fruits of victory of the Chickamauga have now escaped our grasp. The Army of Tennessee, stricken with a complete paralysis, may deem itself fortunate if it escapes from its present position without disaster."

JOINT LETTER FROM BRAXTON BRAGG'S COMMANDERS TO JEFFERSON DAVIS, OCTOBER 4, 1863

For three days following the Battle of Chickamauga a Federal brigade remained on Lookout Mountain, which commanded the main rail and wagon routes to Chattanooga from the west. Then on September 24, over the strong objections of some of his subordinates, a badly shaken Rosecrans decided that the present position was untenable and withdrew the brigade. Braxton Bragg immediately seized the advantage; he occupied Lookout Mountain and posted artillery and sharpshooters along the Tennessee River valley below the ridge, placing Chattanooga under a virtual state of siege.

"The two armies are lying face to face," wrote Union Brigadier General John Beatty. "The Federal and Confederate sentinels walk their beats in sight of each other. The tents of the troops dot the hillsides. We see their signal lights on the summit of Lookout Mountain and on the knobs of Mission Ridge." The overwhelming presence of the Confederates on the height compelled the Federals to devise an alternate supply route into Chattanooga. The Tennessee River was useless. Northwest of the town, in a section of the waterway local residents called The Suck, the stream bed narrowed, creating a current so fierce that no unaided steamer could breast it.

The Federal army had been getting its supplies by rail from Nashville. The trains had run southeast to the settlement of Ste-

venson, Alabama, and thence northeast for a distance of 35 miles along the river to Chattanooga, passing beneath the eminence of Lookout Mountain just before entering the town. After the Confederates occupied the mountain, supplies could be taken by rail only as far as Bridgeport, 27 miles west of Chattanooga. At this junction the Confederates had burned the railroad bridge across the Tennessee River; the route eastward was dominated by their artillery. From Bridgeport, the Federals were forced to take a poor road leading northeast up the valley of the Sequatchie River to Anderson's Crossroads. The wagons then turned southeast — following a steep, winding, rocky trail that was scarcely more than a footpath — over the heights of Walden's Ridge and then down to the north bank of the Tennessee opposite Chattanooga. From that place the wagons moved across the river and into the town over a pontoon bridge.

The 27-mile trip from Bridgeport to Chattanooga by the original rail route took perhaps an hour. The new route, a 60-mile journey, took from eight to 20 days.

The trip was endless in bad weather. Heavy rains fell soon after the battle along the Chickamauga; mules pulling the supply wagons had to struggle up the Sequatchie Valley through stretches of belly-deep mud. On the steep mountain trail as many as 16 animals had to be harnessed to each wagon; a

This forage cap belonged to a sergeant of the 105th Ohio, a unit under siege at Chattanooga. The regiment was in Brigadier General Absalom Baird's division, which suffered severe casualties at Chickamauga. "My loss in killed and wounded," Baird wrote, "attests to the determination with which my men fought."

soldier bearing a whip was assigned to each mule, and more soldiers were put to work pushing. Without question, said a Union officer, the route was "the muddiest and the roughest and steepest of ascent and descent ever crossed by army wagons and mules."

As time passed, the overworked animals weakened until they could barely drag their loads into Chattanooga. Many died en route. Mule carcasses littered the trail all the way from Bridgeport to Chattanooga; "laid lengthwise," said one traveler, "they would easily cover the whole distance."

By the end of September Bragg had decided that his cavalry commander, Major General Joseph Wheeler, should worsen the Federals' plight by attacking their frail and extended line of supply. While making the preparations, Bragg touched off a controversy within the ranks of his officers that was remarkable even for his contentious army. Without any explanation, Bragg instructed General Nathan Bedford Forrest, who had been operating in East Tennessee against Major General Ambrose E. Burnside, to turn over his entire command, with the exception of a single regiment and battery, to Wheeler. On receiving the order the infuriated Forrest went directly to Bragg's headquarters and launched a tirade, the likes of which few army commanders had ever heard from a subordinate officer.

Dr. J. B. Cowan, Forrest's chief surgeon, accompanied him into Bragg's tent. As Cowan recalled it, Forrest ignored Bragg's outstretched hand and announced, "I am not here to pass civilities or compliments with you, but on other business. You commenced your cowardly and contemptible persecution of me soon after the battle of Shiloh and you have kept it up ever since. You did it because

I reported to Richmond facts, while you reported damned lies." Forrest delivered more in this vein, spicing the insults with such epithets as "scoundrel" and "coward," and then produced an appalling climax: "You may as well not issue any more orders to me, for I will not obey them. If you ever again try to interfere with me or cross my path it will be at the peril of your life."

How Braxton Bragg of the incendiary temper replied to this gross insubordination is not recorded. Forrest later took his complaints to President Jefferson Davis and, instead of being punished for his transgressions, was given an independent command in western Tennessee, far from Bragg. Forrest's troopers, however, remained with Bragg and Wheeler.

Meanwhile, on October 1, Wheeler led 5,000 cavalrymen under Brigadier Generals William Martin and John Wharton across the Tennessee River west of Chattanooga and rode north into the Sequatchie Valley. The next day, after destroying a small wagon train, Wheeler sent about half his force northwest under Wharton toward the Federal garrison in McMinnville. Wheeler and Martin then attacked and devastated an 800-wagon Federal caravan at Anderson's Crossroads, burning more than 300 of the vehicles and shooting or sabering the mules.

Federal cavalry was in hot pursuit. Brigadier General George Crook's division closed from the northeast, while Colonel Edward M. McCook's division came north from Bridgeport. McCook was first on the scene, with two regiments. Theodore Davis, a writer and artist for *Harper's Illustrated Weekly*, was with McCook's troops. He wrote that as they approached Anderson's Crossroads, they saw "a dense smoke, caused by the

burning of a large wagon train. At three o'clock we came upon the enemy, charging them at once. The rebels drew up in line, fired one volley, then turned and ran, dropping their plunder as they went."

The Confederates drew up successive lines of battle, only to be dispersed by the Federal saber charges. Davis related that during one of these charges Wheeler himself narrowly escaped: "Colonel La Grange of the 1st Wisconsin had cut down one of Wheeler's staff, run his trusty blade through another, and dashed at Wheeler, whom he had nearly reached, when the rebel jumped his horse over a fence, which the horse of the gallant Colonel refused." McCook inflicted almost 300 casualties on the raiders and recaptured some wagons and mules. Crook's division, meanwhile, had pursued Wharton to McMinnville, but not fast enough. The town fell to the Confederates on October 3. Crook

succeeded in blocking Wharton's progress farther west toward Murfreesboro; by October 7 all of Wheeler's troops were withdrawing south, pursued by the now-consolidated Federal divisions.

By the time Wheeler's Confederates got back across the Tennessee River they had suffered damaging losses, totaling at least 700 killed or wounded. They had nevertheless hurt the Federals badly. Wheeler had destroyed several railroad bridges, about 500 wagons and, most seriously for the besieged Federals, more than a thousand mules.

The destruction of so many draft animals greatly increased the burden on those remaining — just as Wheeler had intended. Desperately needed supplies were dumped on the trail to lighten the loads; otherwise the wagons might not have gotten through at all.

Miscalculations threw supply into confusion. On one occasion the mountain route

General Wheeler and his troopers seize a Federal supply train in a daring raid near Anderson's Crossroads. Some of the Confederates found what must have been a sutler's wagon; an observer wrote that the gleeful men "waded up to their necks in fine $50 hats, $100 boots, rivers of Champagne and liquors of all kinds, pyramids of cigars, fruits, jellies and every sort of luxury."

Major General Joseph (Fighting Joe) Wheeler, one of the Confederacy's best cavalry commanders, was known for his aggressiveness and innovation in combat. In 1863 he published *Cavalry Tactics*, which advocated the revolutionary use of troopers fighting dismounted with infantry rifles.

became so filled with wagons trying to reach Chattanooga that there was no room for empty wagons trying to get back. A colossal traffic jam resulted. "Five hundred teams," reported Charles Dana, "were halted between the mountain and the river without forage for the animals, and unable to move in any direction; the whole road was strewn with dead animals." John K. Duke, an enlisted man with the 53rd Ohio, wrote that when one mule went off the path, "hanging over a precipice, endangering the other mules of the team, it was cut loose, and dropped 200-300 feet below."

As the siege wore on, it became more and more difficult to feed the mules, along the trail or in Chattanooga. Half-starved, they chewed on trees, fences, wagons and any-

thing else they could reach. That autumn, 10,000 draft animals died.

The people in the town were not much better off. Food in Chattanooga grew so scarce that men stole corn from the horses or hunted for it on the ground where the animals had eaten. "I have often seen hundreds of soldiers following behind the wagon trains which had just arrived," said correspondent W.F.G. Shanks of the New York *Herald*, "picking out of the mud the crumbs of bread, coffee, rice, etc., which were wasted from the boxes and sacks by the rattling of the wagons over the stones."

By mid-October, officers frequently were being assailed by cries of "Crackers!" from men who were now eager to see more of the usually despised hardtack. There was much conjecture about when a new supply route — a "Cracker Line" — might be opened to relieve the siege.

The civilians suffered most of all. While the Army command was making some effort, however inadequate, to feed the soldiers, the noncombatants had no one to help them. They were not only hungry but miserable, living in squalor in what had once been a pretty, prosperous town. The civilian residents of Chattanooga and the 35,000 men of the Army of the Cumberland were jammed together in an area of about one square mile. The civilians, their houses having been torn down to provide fuel for the campfires, were crowded into the center of this enclave. Their shacks, recalled Shanks, "surpassed in filth, numbers of occupants and general destitution the worst tenements in New York City." Most of the civilians eventually fled the town, picking their way painfully north over Walden's Ridge. An officer reported encountering ill-clad women and children on

Federal soldiers in winter quarters at Chattanooga form up behind a makeshift fence; wallpaper on the boards attests to the scarcity of wood in the besieged town: Union soldiers tore down houses and used the scavenged planks as firewood and building material.

the trail "exposed to the beatings of the storm, wet and shivering with cold. I have seen much of misery consequent upon this war," he said, "but never before in so distressing a form as this."

Amid all this hardship — and with worse trouble threatening — Rosecrans, said Dana, seemed "dazed and mazy" and "insensible to the impending danger." Although the commanding general ordered that steamboats be built and the railroads repaired, he had no concrete plan.

Rosecrans did take the time to apportion blame for the defeat at Chickamauga: Soon after the battle he removed Generals Alexander McCook and Thomas Crittenden from command of their corps for having left the field after Longstreet's attack. Their units were combined to form a new IV Corps under the command of Major General Gordon Granger. (A court of inquiry later cleared both McCook and Crittenden of any responsibility for the Federal rout.)

Rosecrans' action against the two generals did nothing to distract attention from his own deterioration. Lincoln was well aware of the situation: Dana was sending reports critical of Rosecrans to Secretary of War Edwin M. Stanton, which the Secretary was sharing with the President. "The practical incapacity of the general commanding is astonishing," Dana wrote, "and it often seems difficult to believe him of sound mind."

Lincoln did what he could to shore up the unsteady Chattanooga commander and assured him of Washington's continued support. And General in Chief Henry W. Halleck continued to rush reinforcements into the area. Major General Joseph Hooker, who had been inactive since his shattering defeat at Chancellorsville five months before, was

sent west with Major General Henry W. Slocum's XII Corps and Major General Oliver O. Howard's XI Corps — a unit whose poor performance at Chancellorsville and Gettysburg had earned it the worst reputation in the army. Dispatched by train from Virginia on September 25, Hooker got the lead elements of his 20,000-man command to Bridgeport in only six days — a considerable achievement of logistics. Once there, however, Hooker could do little: To march into Chattanooga would serve only to add his men to the 35,000 soldiers already starving there. Hooker based his troops on Bridgeport and strung them back along the railroad to protect the line. Then he waited.

Four more divisions, under Major General William Tecumseh Sherman, had been sent east from Memphis and Vicksburg before the Battle of Chickamauga. But Halleck had ordered them to repair the Memphis & Charleston Railroad as they marched so that they could supply themselves. As a consequence they made little progress.

In any case, it was becoming increasingly evident to the President that no amount of reinforcement would solve the problem in Chattanooga. General Rosecrans was clearly unable to come to grips with the difficulties confronting him; Lincoln said the general was "stunned and confused, like a duck hit on the head."

At the same time, the Confederate command structure was also embroiled in controversy. Braxton Bragg, like his opposite number Rosecrans, had followed the Battle of Chickamauga with a purge of supposedly errant officers. Blaming General Leonidas Polk for the delay on the morning of the battle's second day, Bragg relieved him and sent him to

Atlanta to await orders. Bragg also sacked General Thomas Hindman for missing the opportunity to trap General James Negley's division at McLemore's Cove the week before the battle proper.

In self-defense, Bragg's subordinates were attempting once again to have him replaced as commander of the Army of Tennessee. Arrayed against Bragg was a formidable roster of generals, headed by James Longstreet, Polk, Daniel Harvey Hill and Simon Buckner, all corps commanders. On October 4 these officers — and eight other generals commanding divisions or brigades — sent a formal petition to Jefferson Davis urging Bragg's removal. "The fruits of the victory at Chickamauga have now escaped our grasp," the petitioners said; the army was "stricken with a complete paralysis." They attributed this situation to the poor state of Bragg's health, which they said "unfits him for the command of an army in the field."

Davis was deeply disturbed by the petition and the command problems that it revealed. First, he interceded on behalf of Polk, whom he liked. But Bragg refused to reinstate Polk; instead he preferred formal charges against him. These were dropped by the War Department and Polk was restored to his command, but he would not serve any longer under Bragg. "I certainly feel a lofty contempt for his puny effort to inflict injury upon a man who has dry-nursed him," Polk wrote to his daughter.

Then, as the uproar grew increasingly virulent, President Davis boarded a train for the long journey — via the Carolinas and Georgia — to Bragg's headquarters outside Chattanooga. When he arrived on October 9, a crowd of soldiers cheered and bands played. There were cries of "Speech!" but

General Ulysses S. Grant, though impeccably uniformed in this photograph, usually paid scant attention to his appearance. A fellow officer wrote at the time that Grant "wore his uniform more like a civilian than a graduate of West Point. Neither his face nor his figure was imposing."

Davis declined gracefully. "Man never spoke as you did on the field of Chickamauga," he told the soldiers, "and in your presence I dare not speak." But later he did make a speech, in which he chided the army for its poor opinion of its commander. The troops, President Davis said, should crown their achievements with "harmony, due subordination and cheerful support to lawful authority."

On the night that he arrived, Davis presided over one of the oddest councils of the War. Except for Polk, whose place was taken by Major General Benjamin F. Cheatham, all the corps commanders were present — as was Bragg, of course — and after a discussion of the military situation Davis asked for comment on Bragg's fitness to command. Since Bragg himself was there, staring stonily at the wall, the situation was extremely uncomfortable. When Davis insisted on a response, Longstreet declared, as he later recalled, "that our commander could be of greater service elsewhere." The other corps commanders concurred.

On this uneasy note the meeting ended. Bragg must have been profoundly embarrassed, but he knew something the other officers did not: Before the session Davis had assured Bragg that he would not be relieved of command. Davis was one of the few people who genuinely liked the irascible general. Besides, the President could not come up with anyone to replace Bragg as commander of the Army of Tennessee. Even before leaving Richmond, Davis had concluded that there was no one else to whom he could entrust the command.

Davis departed a few days later, having addressed the command problems simply by demoting or replacing all those opposed to Bragg. In the process the Army of Tennessee was reorganized into three corps. Polk was assigned to General Joseph E. Johnston's Alabama-Mississippi department in exchange for Lieutenant General William J. Hardee, who returned to the Army of Tennessee as a corps commander. Simon Buckner was reduced from corps commander to division commander and was soon after granted a leave of absence. Daniel Harvey Hill was suspended and sent home, and his corps was turned over to Major General John C. Breckinridge — who was an implacable foe of Bragg's, but who had not signed the petition that sought his removal. Bragg then relented in one case, returning Thomas Hindman to command under Breckinridge.

It was obviously impossible to dispose so easily of James Longstreet, one of the most respected generals in the entire Confederate Army. Longstreet was stripped of several divisions — he kept only his two from Virginia — but neither Davis nor Bragg could have demoted the general without setting off a furor throughout the Confederacy. However, Davis had thought of an assignment, which for the present he shared only with Bragg, that soon would separate the squabbling officers — with fateful consequences.

In the second week of October, about the time Jefferson Davis arrived in the Confederate camp, Major General Ulysses S. Grant in Vicksburg received a mysterious communication from General in Chief Halleck. It instructed him to travel to Cairo, Illinois, and upon his arrival there to report by telegraph to Washington. Halleck offered no explanation.

Grant had spent a frustrating summer. Immediately after accepting the surrender of

Vicksburg he had proposed to Washington that his army, which had been reinforced for the Vicksburg siege, move against Mobile, Alabama, a major strategic objective. The proposal was rejected, and instead Grant spent the stifling hot summer months building new defensive works around Vicksburg.

In September Grant traveled down the Mississippi to New Orleans to confer with Major General Nathaniel P. Banks, commander of the Department of the Gulf. And there misfortune struck Grant. On the third day of his visit he was honored by a review, and afterward he and Banks and a number of other officers attended an elegant dinner — with "music, wine, choruses, etc.," a participant recalled — at a New Orleans restaurant. Returning from this affair Grant, a first-class horseman, was riding a spirited, unfamiliar animal; challenged by his mount, he sped ahead of the others. As he approached a railroad track, a passing locomotive emitted a loud whistle. The horse, already nearly unmanageable, reared, fell on Grant and knocked him senseless. When he came to, he was being attended by doctors in a hotel room. "My leg," he wrote later, "was swollen from the knee to the thigh, and the swelling, almost to the point of bursting, extended along the body to the armpit."

As always when something unusual happened to Grant, there were suggestions that he was drunk. Indeed, the rumors of Grant's drinking that day were supported by a few firsthand allegations. Banks wrote his wife that Grant's inebriation "was too manifest to all who saw him." Major General William B. Franklin also said he had seen Grant drunk at the time of the accident.

In any case, his leg and side had been severely bruised. Grant spent 14 days in bed

Men of General Thomas' corps stand to within a maze of fortifications protecting the city of Chattanooga. Although Confederate gun crews occasionally lobbed shells from Lookout Mountain (background), there was little urgency to their efforts: General Bragg was convinced that it was "only a question of time" before the Federal army was starved into submission.

and then returned to Vicksburg to continue convalescing; on September 25 he finally tried getting about on crutches and found that he was very weak. Nevertheless, he reported to Halleck on September 28 that he was "ready for the field." Two weeks later, following Halleck's mysterious instructions, Grant was on his way to Cairo.

When he arrived there and sent word to Washington on October 16 he received a new set of equally enigmatic orders: "You will immediately proceed to the Galt House, Louisville, Kentucky, where you will meet an officer of the War Department with your orders and instructions. You will take with you your staff, etc., for immediate operations in the field."

The "officer of the War Department" who greeted Grant — he actually boarded Grant's train in Indianapolis — turned out to be none other than Secretary of War Edwin Stanton. The Secretary and Grant had never met and, as usual, Grant's shabby appearance belied his rank. After Stanton bustled into Grant's railroad car at the Indianapolis station he shook hands with Dr. Edward Kittoe, Grant's staff surgeon, and said: "How are you, General Grant? I knew you at sight from your pictures."

Once Stanton had located the real Grant, he handed him two sets of orders and told him to choose between them. Both sets decreed a radical change in the chain of command in the West. The three armies operating in the Tennessee area — the Armies of the Cumberland, the Ohio and the Tennessee (Grant's old Vicksburg command) — would be incorporated in a new Military Division of the Mississippi under Grant. Now came the choice: One set of orders left Rosecrans in command of the Army of the Cum-

berland; the other named General George H. Thomas as Rosecrans' replacement.

Grant had certain reservations about Thomas; he considered him to be too slow. But he regarded Rosecrans as even more deliberate and a good deal less reliable. Grant did not hesitate. He replaced Rosecrans with General Thomas.

Grant and Stanton spent October 19 in Louisville talking strategy. That night the Secretary received an alarming — although inaccurate — message from Charles Dana: Rosecrans was making preparations to abandon Chattanooga. Greatly upset, Stanton instructed Grant that under no circumstances was the Army of the Cumberland to withdraw from the town.

Grant instantly sent off a flurry of telegrams notifying Rosecrans and Thomas of the changes in command and ordering Thomas to "Hold Chattanooga at all hazards." The reply from the Rock of Chickamauga was immediate: "We will hold the town till we starve."

Then Grant set out at all speed for Chattanooga. When he reached the railroad junction at Stevenson, Alabama, he met General Rosecrans, who was on his way home to Cincinnati. The two men had a cordial meeting. "He described very clearly the situation at Chattanooga," Grant recalled, "and made some excellent suggestions as to what should be done." Grant then added dryly: "My only wonder was that he had not carried them out."

Grant's journey from Bridgeport to Chattanooga over the long Federal supply route through Anderson's Crossroads revealed to him the seriousness of the problems he faced. A driving downpour persisted for the entire trip. The steep, narrow and slippery road, Grant wrote, "was strewn with the debris of broken wagons and the carcasses of thousands of starved mules and horses." At one point, Grant's horse slipped on the treacherous trail and threw him; his battered leg was again severely bruised.

On October 23 just as darkness was falling, Grant arrived at Thomas' headquarters "wet, dirty and well," in Dana's words. Grant found that despite his fall the hard traveling had improved, rather than worsened, his injured leg. Early the next morning Grant was back on his horse, studying the terrain and listening delightedly to a plan — already set in motion by Thomas — for ending the Confederate siege.

The author of the plan was a West Point acquaintance of Grant's, Brigadier General William F. Smith. He had joined the Army of the Cumberland as its chief engineer only a few days before. Already his men had built a sawmill — using, said Grant, "an old engine found in the neighborhood" — and were building crude boats and pontoons.

Smith had made a careful study of the area's geography, with special attention to the terrain between the army at Chattanooga and its supply base at Bridgeport. Two and a half miles downstream from Chattanooga, the Tennessee River interrupted its southwestward course and made an abrupt turn to the northwest around a tongue of land called Moccasin Point. From the pontoon bridge already in place at Chattanooga a road led directly westward across Moccasin Point for two miles until it hit the river again at Brown's Ferry.

From Brown's Ferry the river continued northwestward for five miles toward Walden's Ridge then made another hairpin turn to the southwest for seven miles, creating a peninsula open to the south. The road from Brown's Ferry continued west across this neck of land to another ferry — Kelley's. Significantly, Kelley's Ferry could be reached from Bridgeport by steamboat.

The road from Chattanooga to Kelley's Ferry was for its entire length out of range of the Confederate artillery posted on Lookout Mountain. The problem was that the Confederates were holding Brown's Ferry and a stretch of road west of it.

By taking control of that short stretch the Federals could get their supplies into Chattanooga with an overland haul of only eight miles. And Smith had a plan.

Two forces would move against Brown's Ferry from Chattanooga, one marching straight across Moccasin Point while the other — the key to the operation — drifted down the river in pontoon boats. The water-borne force would surprise and overpower the pickets on the Confederate side of the river. Then the combined forces would use the pontoons to build a bridge and move on to occupy the road to Kelley's Ferry.

In addition General Joseph Hooker was to send three of his divisions across the Tennessee on pontoons at Bridgeport. They were to march eastward along the railroad, around the flanks of the lightly held Raccoon Mountain to the hamlet of Wauhatchie, just west of Lookout Mountain. There, Hooker's men would be in a position to support the attacks on the ferries, if necessary, and could also help clear the area between them.

Grant endorsed the plan enthusiastically. The preparations were made in strictest secrecy, and at 3 a.m. on the 27th Smith's forces moved stealthily out of the town. While 3,500 infantrymen commanded by Brigadier General John B. Turchin marched overland toward Confederate-held Brown's Ferry with three batteries of artillery in support, Brigadier General William B. Hazen and 1,500 more troops floated noiselessly down the Tennessee in 50 oar-equipped pontoons and two flatboats.

Once past the Chattanooga defenses, the Federal soldiers on the water were in enemy territory and would be for seven miles; there was a full moon, but a light fog and scattered clouds helped hide them. For two tense hours they drifted downriver, the men lying flat in their boats, motionless and soundless. Hazen's troops could hear the Confederate sentinels singing to keep themselves awake; and at one point two guards could be seen staring intently over the river toward the boats—but no alarm was given.

As the sky began to lighten, the leading pontoons came abreast of some small signal fires lit on the east bank by Turchin's men. The silence was shattered as General Hazen bellowed "Pull in!" The men in the boats sprang up, their squad leaders shouted orders, the oars were unlimbered—and the handful of Confederate pickets on the west bank opened fire.

The Federals hit the west bank and scrambled ashore in the dim light, more or less at their assigned places near the ferry landing; and they were able to brush away the enemy pickets easily. But the road ahead ran in a defile through a steep ridge that commanded the ferry landing; the men would have to take the crest of that ridge if they expected to hold the bridgehead. And that was not going to be easy.

There were six Confederate companies on the height, and they were commanded by one of Longstreet's most promising young officers, Colonel William C. Oates. Hearing

Having earlier been relieved of command for insubordination, General William F. (Baldy) Smith (*above*) retrieved a measure of favor in planning the surprise assault on Brown's Ferry, which was carried out by General William B. Hazen (*left*).

gunfire and informed of the routing of the pickets, he ordered two of his companies to counterattack immediately. Oates recalled that he told his officers "to deploy their men at one pace apart and instruct them to walk right up to the foe, and for every man to place the muzzle of his rifle against the body of a Yankee when he fired."

Employing this unusual tactic as best they could, two of Oates's companies were able to drive back the Federals for a distance, but soon they were receiving heavy fire from the flank. Finally, Oates sent in all six of his companies, he wrote, "and still I could not cover the enemy's front." While encouraging his men, Oates was felled by a bullet in the right hip.

During this skirmish Turchin's Federals were using the pontoon boats to row

Gliding silently past the Confederate outposts, General Hazen's troops prepare to land their pontoon boats at Brown's Ferry. Lashing their craft together, the Federals constructed a bridge over the Tennessee River and established a new supply line by midafternoon.

ment Brownt Ferry
27-14 1863 Opening the Cracker * a To Chattanooga.

themselves across the river, and soon they possessed overwhelming odds. Outflanked and outnumbered, the Confederates withdrew to the south, toward Lookout Mountain, carrying Colonel Oates with them. The Federal forces secured the bridgehead and went to work.

By midafternoon of the 27th, the pontoons had been planked over to make a serviceable bridge at Brown's Ferry, protected by light breastworks. The little operation had been accomplished without a hitch. Federal casualties totaled 38; only six of them were fatali-

ties. An exultant General Hazen strode along his lines yelling to his men, "We've knocked the cover off the cracker box!"

Federal reinforcements were on the way. Hooker had started his troops east toward Chattanooga that morning. Major General Oliver O. Howard led the way with the two XI Corps divisions; Brigadier General John W. Geary followed with a division from Slocum's XII Corps. Their advance was almost completely without incident, and by evening on the 28th Howard's men were in position a mile from Brown's Ferry. General

Geary's division halted three miles to the south, in Wauhatchie.

The Confederate high command was slow to react to this critical development. Despite repeated warnings from Oates and others, Longstreet apparently believed that the action at Brown's Ferry was of little significance, and he did not even bother to pass the word to Bragg. When Bragg learned of the rout, he was furious; and on the morning of October 28 he summoned Longstreet to a conference on Lookout Mountain. As the two men argued heatedly, a signal party sent word that Federal columns were approaching from the southwest. Bragg refused to believe the report, but then he and Longstreet were led to a place that afforded a sweeping view of the valley. Longstreet recalled later

that they could see the Federals on the road below "marching quietly along the valley toward Brown's Ferry." As they watched, Geary's division "came in sight and made its bivouac immediately in front of the point where we stood."

Even though the threat was now obvious, Bragg and Longstreet apparently failed to agree on a course of action. Bragg insisted that Longstreet attack the Federal bridgehead at Brown's Ferry, using both of his divisions; Bragg even made available an additional division of Breckinridge's corps as a reserve. But it appears that Longstreet had other ideas: Instead he advanced on Geary's troops at Wauhatchie with a single division in a rare night attack.

Longstreet dispatched Hood's former di-

In this ghostly battlescape, Federal troops under Brigadier General John Geary hold their ground *(rear right)* as the Confederates attempt to recapture Brown's Ferry on the night of October 28. Geary fought off the attack successfully, but not without great personal cost: His son, Edward, was killed in the battle.

vision, now under Brigadier General Micah Jenkins, west past the tip of Lookout Mountain to the road linking Wauhatchie and Brown's Ferry. From there a brigade under Brigadier General Evander M. Law moved a short distance to the north and took a position on high ground to the right of the road to prevent Hooker's main force from reinforcing Geary. Jenkins took a brigade of 1,800 men south and, shortly after midnight, deployed and advanced on Geary.

There was a strong moon that night, but frequently it was obscured by drifting clouds. The Confederates attacked in a rush, out of the darkness. "The enemy precipitately hurled his main body, without skirmishers, on my left," General Geary wrote afterward. Although Geary was more experienced as a politician—elected Mayor of San Francisco and later Governor of Kansas—than as a general, he commanded his men well. Despite the shock of the sudden assault, the Federals stood fast. No one was able to see more than a few feet into the darkness. According to a soldier serving with the 149th New York, "the fire of the men was directed by watching the explosion of the enemy's muskets."

Geary's defenders had two advantages. They knew approximately where their lines were and therefore could shoot without hitting comrades. And they had four guns already positioned to fire over their own lines into the enemy's.

As the engagement spread from Geary's left to his right, he could hear the attackers calling to one another to "pick off the artillerists." As a fierce new attack was launched on Geary's right flank, two companies of the 111th Pennsylvania and one gun—under Geary's son, Lieutenant Edward Geary—

were repositioned to meet it. The Pennsylvanians held, but the Federals paid a stiff price: General Geary reported that "it was under this fire that my men fell rapidly and the battery suffered a most unparalleled loss." Two of the Federal guns were put out of commission, and Geary's son was killed. The devout Geary wrote later of his son's death: "I trust in this chastisement. Oh, my God, I feel this chastisement for the pride I took in him."

Their losses notwithstanding, the embattled Federals continued to fight off Jenkins' Confederates. General Hooker, at Brown's Ferry, had heard the firing and had ordered a division commanded by Major General Carl Schurz to rush to Geary's relief at the double-quick. The other division, under Brigadier General Adolph von Steinwehr, was to follow. Schurz's division started off down the wrong road and got lost in a swamp but eventually found its way to Wauhatchie and ran into Law's waiting Confederates. At this point the Federals fell into bungling. Apparently the orders that instructed at least a part of the force to continue to Wauhatchie to join Geary either were not delivered or were not obeyed. Two Federal brigades—one of Schurz's and later one of von Steinwehr's—stopped to deal with Law, but the bulk of the Federal reinforcements—four brigades—unaccountably halted, leaving Geary to fight his own battle.

Law's Confederates were well situated on high ground. Although outnumbered and even almost encircled by their enemy, they were able to withstand several Federal attacks and inflict heavy casualties. Finally, a brigade of von Steinwehr's division launched a bayonet charge, in the dark, up the rugged hill in a last-ditch effort to dislodge the Con-

An actual sketch, made on the spot by one of the Special Artists of Frank Leslie's Illustrated Newspaper.

Mr. Leslie holds the copyright and reserves the exclusive right of publication.

Federal steamboat slips through an opening in the pontoon bridge at Brown's Ferry. The Federal "Cracker Line" — so called for the hardtack carried over it — was a combination land and water route that traversed the Tennessee in three places, far out of range of Confederate guns.

The makeshift steamboat *Chattanooga* lies moored to the bank of the Tennessee River, its decks laden with sacks of grain. The vessel was the first to run the Cracker Line. Lacking any other supply boat, builders in Bridgeport worked feverishly to construct the *Chattanooga;* then, struggling with bad weather and frequent breakdowns, a crew brought it upstream loaded with vital supplies.

federates. The reckless ascent was led by the 33rd Massachusetts under Lieutenant Colonel Godfrey Rider Jr. Advancing under heavy fire, the Massachusetts men soon reached a formidable obstacle — as Rider described it, "a crooked ravine some 20 feet deep, the sides of which were almost perpendicular, slippery with leaves and clay, and covered with brush rendered still more formidable by the deceptive moonlight.

"The regiment gallantly plunged into it," Rider continued, "the dead and living rolling down together." The troops fell back under heavy fire, re-formed and advanced again with fixed bayonets. The hill became so steep that in some places the men had to pull themselves up by grasping shrubs and roots. Reaching the crest, Rider's men charged into the Confederates, who broke and fled down the opposite slope. A captured soldier told the Federals that he and his comrades were disgraced by their retreat but, "you kept coming, and the next we knew you were right among us."

By this time Geary, too, was contemplating a bayonet charge; he was almost out of ammunition, and his flanks had been pushed back until the men on the right were standing almost back to back with the men on the left. But it was the Confederates who gave out first. Suddenly, Geary wrote, "at half past three o'clock they ceased firing on our left, their hostility manifestly having grown weaker during the last fifteen minutes, and, firing a few volleys at our center, which were promptly responded to, they retired, leaving the field in our possession."

Afterward a rumor circulated in the Federal camp that the Confederates had broken off the engagement under highly unusual circumstances. As the tale went, the teamsters accompanying Geary's division had panicked when the battle started, abandoning their mules. Later the frightened animals stampeded into the Confederate lines — "heads down and tails up," according to an alleged witness, "with trace chains rattling and whiffletrees snapping over the stumps of trees." Some of the startled Confederates, sure they were facing a cavalry charge, faltered and fled.

The story of the mule attack was told and retold in the Federal army, doubtless improving with each retelling. As it happened, the battle had occurred at a time when the Northern public believed that too many brevet, or honorary, promotions were being handed out. General Grant was greatly amused, reported an officer, when the quartermaster whose department was in charge of the mules forwarded the following recommendation to him: "I respectfully request that the mules, for their gallantry in this action, may have conferred upon them the brevet rank of horses."

With Longstreet's withdrawal from Wauhatchie and the Lookout Valley, the Federal Cracker Line was at last open. Grant dispatched reinforcements to protect the newly won route; in short order there were more than 20,000 Federal troops south of the Tennessee River and west of Lookout Mountain, and Braxton Bragg could no longer maintain the siege of Chattanooga.

On October 29, a makeshift steamboat pulling two barges loaded with rations and forage started up the Tennessee River from Bridgeport against the powerful current. Time after time the decrepit engine broke down, and the vessel drifted backward. But "we kept on," reported William G. Le Duc,

Situated on the Nashville & Chattanooga Railroad line, Anderson, Tennessee, became a supply depot for the trapped Federal army in Chattanooga. From Anderson, supply trains would cross Big Crow Creek (*foreground*) and proceed to Bridgeport, the start of the Cracker Line.

the officer in charge, "trembling and hoping." All night through a driving rain the little boat churned painfully upstream "like a blind person," said Le Duc. By dawn, the craft was tied up at Kelley's Ferry. A soldier heard cheering and hurried over to find out why. "Has Grant come?" he asked a man on the landing. "Grant be damned!" said the man. "A boatload of rations has come!" In Chattanooga, said Le Duc, "there were but four boxes of hard bread left in the commissary warehouses."

One load, of course, was not enough, and Grant moved quickly to get supplies flowing into Chattanooga. He instructed the superintendent of military railroads to send at least 30 carloads of rations daily from Nashville to Bridgeport; "the road," he said, "must be run to its utmost capacity." Still, the single line of track that ran between Chattanooga and the main Federal base at Nashville likely would be inadequate to carry all the supplies the army needed.

Grant had a solution in mind. Another rail line led south from Nashville to Decatur, Alabama; from there the Memphis & Charleston line ran eastward to Chattanooga. It was a roundabout route, and the track had been wrecked almost beyond hope by Confederate cavalry and guerrillas, but Grant would have another access to his supply base if he could repair the rails. To provide the muscle for the mammoth job, Grant looked to General William Tecumseh Sherman's troops. Sherman had been making his way slowly eastward from Memphis, repairing the railroad as Halleck had ordered. It was an impossible task; the road ran through hostile country, and often Sherman's work was destroyed as soon as he finished it. On November 3 Grant ordered Sherman to abandon his position

and move his troops forward. To oversee the rebuilding project Grant named Brigadier General Grenville M. Dodge, a division commander under Sherman.

In civilian life Dodge had been a railroad surveyor and engineer, and he was accustomed to difficult assignments. But he had never been given a more awesome task than this one. "The road from Nashville to Decatur passes over a broken country," Grant wrote later, "cut up with innumerable streams, many of them of considerable width, and with valleys far below the road bed. All the bridges over these had been destroyed, and the rails taken up and twisted by the enemy. All bridges and culverts had been destroyed between Nashville and Decatur, and thence to Stevenson."

No fewer than 182 bridges had to be rebuilt and no less than 102 miles of track restored. Yet by working at an astonishing rate — repairing more than four bridges and two and a half miles of track a day — Dodge and his troops reconstructed the entire line in only 40 days.

During that time, the Federal forces in Chattanooga continued to subsist at the ragged edge of hunger. The most that could be said, Grant acknowledged, was that "actual suffering was prevented." And the problem remained of replacing the thousands of horses and mules that had perished in the Confederate siege.

On November 13 General Sherman arrived in Bridgeport with the advance of his troops. Shortly thereafter he went with Grant to inspect the fortifications facing the Confederate lines at Chattanooga. "All along Missionary Ridge were the tents of the rebel beleaguering force," Sherman wrote later.

"The lines of trench from Lookout up toward the Chickamauga were plainly visible; and rebel sentinels, in a continuous chain, were walking their posts in plain view, not a thousand yards off. 'Why,' said I, 'General Grant you are besieged'; and he said, 'It is too true.' Up to that moment I had no idea that things were so bad."

There was some desultory firing between the lines, but it rarely assumed major proportions. Both sides were suffering from an ammunition shortage. When Grant had arrived he found that Thomas' men had barely enough ammunition for one day's fighting. On the Confederate side, there were so few cartridges that in at least one unit any soldier who fired his musket without receiving permission was fined 25 cents.

Curiously, the Confederates were enduring privations almost as severe as those suffered by the soldiers they had entrapped. Supplies were available, but the Confederate distribution system had broken down. Kentuckian John Green complained that his rations consisted of cornmeal that contained "a good deal of the cob," plus "the poorest kind of blue beef."

Living conditions for the Confederates were often abysmal. "The army was in a bad way," wrote Captain Fitzgerald Ross, an Austrian Army officer and visitor to Bragg's camp. "Insufficiently sheltered, and contin-

Union soldiers, sporting jaunty, non-regulation neckerchiefs, exude confidence as they stand shoulder to shoulder at Chattanooga's rail depot after the siege of the city was lifted.

ually drenched with rain, the men were seldom able to dry their clothes; and a great deal of sickness was the natural consequence." Blankets were scarce, he said, and tents scarcer. One of Longstreet's officers observed sourly: "There is a tradition amongst these flats that there has been a time in the past when it wasn't raining." The ground, he said, "is knee-deep in mud and slush, and the air so dark and dank that it may be cut with a knife."

During the lull, fraternization became commonplace, in spite of the rules against it. Brigadier General John Beatty reported that "the pickets of the two armies are growing quite intimate, sitting about on logs together, talking over the great battle, and exchanging views as to the results of a future engagement."

Private Sam Watkins, a Tennessean in Bragg's army, witnessed a riverside encounter between a Confederate sergeant and a Federal soldier; the two men had become such good friends that the sergeant invited the Northerner to cross the river. The Federal waded through the waist-deep water to the opposite shore. They "swapped a few lies, canteens and tobacco," and then the Union soldier waded back. Only later did the Confederates discover that their Northern visitor had been none other than Colonel John Wilder, exploring possible river crossings for his Lightning Brigade.

Grant himself became involved in some fraternization one day when he rode down to a stream that provided drinking water to both sides. As he approached, a Federal picket called out, "Turn out the guard for the commanding general." Not wanting to attract attention, Grant said hastily, "Never mind the guard," and the men returned to their tents. At that moment, there came a cry from the Confederate sentinel across the creek: "Turn out the guard for the commanding general," and Grant thought he heard his own name mentioned. "Their line in a moment fronted to the north, facing me," wrote Grant with obvious relish, "and gave me a salute, which I returned."

Grant also paused for a brief exchange with a blue-clad Confederate. "He was very polite," Grant recalled, "and, touching his hat to me, said he belonged to General Longstreet's corps. I asked him a few questions—but not with a view of gaining any particular information—all of which he answered, and I rode off."

Grant did not mention the date of this encounter, but it must have been in late October: By November 5, Longstreet and his men were gone from Bragg's army. As Jefferson Davis had suggested a few weeks before, Longstreet was dispatched on a mission of dubious strategic wisdom—to head for Knoxville and destroy Ambrose Burnside's little Army of the Ohio.

The Contest for Knoxville

"Their march was over dead and wounded comrades, yet still they faltered not, but onward, still onward. Over the prostrate bodies marched the doomed heroes of that forlorn hope."

NORTHERN CORRESPONDENT, OF THE CONFEDERATE CHARGE ON FORT SANDERS

"If the rebels give me one week more time," Ulysses S. Grant wired General in Chief Halleck after the fight at Wauhatchie, "all danger of losing territory now held by us will have passed away and preparations may commence for offensive operations." Incredibly, Braxton Bragg not only gave the Federals time but obligingly weakened his own army by ordering General James Longstreet north to attack Major General Ambrose E. Burnside at Knoxville. The strategy was poor; but it did remove from Bragg's sight another general who thought him unfit for command. Longstreet's departure, Bragg wrote to Jefferson Davis on October 31, "will be a great relief to me."

Longstreet was appalled by the order. His force numbered 10,000 infantrymen — the divisions of Major General Lafayette McLaws and Brigadier General Micah Jenkins — along with Major General Joseph Wheeler's 5,000 cavalrymen. Without more men he had little hope of prevailing against Burnside's superior forces: 12,000 infantry plus 8,500 cavalry. Yet Longstreet's departure would leave the Army of Tennessee with about 40,000 men along an eight-mile line facing a concentrated enemy that with General William Sherman's arrival would number almost 60,000. By separating the Confederate forces, Longstreet argued, "We thus expose both to failure, and really take no chance to ourselves of great results."

Before leaving, Longstreet tried to persuade Bragg to abandon the overextended lines around Chattanooga and move the army farther south in a better defensive position. From the new location, Longstreet could strike across the Tennessee River and sever Grant's lines of communication. Bragg replied with a sardonic smile; Longstreet had his instructions. Any further discussion would be "out of order."

As his men packed to move north on November 5, Longstreet wrote a note to General Simon Bolivar Buckner asking for any information the general could offer about the Knoxville area. Longstreet gloomily concluded in the note that "it was to be the fate of our army to wait until all good opportunities had passed, and then, in desperation, seize upon the least favorable movement."

The events of the next few days deepened Longstreet's discouragement. The trains that were to carry his men to Sweetwater, roughly midway between Chattanooga and Knoxville, failed to arrive. Longstreet, tired of waiting, started his troops toward Knoxville on foot, hoping their transport would catch up with them.

Those trains that finally appeared along the route were, said staff officer Colonel Moxley Sorrel, "almost comical in their inefficiency." The locomotives were so decrepit that they could not pull the cars up some of the grades with the soldiers aboard. "When a hill was reached," said Sorrel, "the long train would be instantly emptied — platforms, roofs, doors, and windows — of our fellows, like ants out of a hill." The men

This wood-shell drum was used by Confederate troops during the Knoxville Campaign. The soldiers' day began with bugle and drum calls, and veteran troops were able to maneuver by drumbeat alone, without any verbal instruction.

would trudge along the tracks to the summit, and there they would pile on board again. It took eight days for all of Longstreet's men to travel the 60 or so miles to Sweetwater.

A fresh blow awaited Longstreet there. He had been led to believe that supplies would be available at Sweetwater. His men were on short rations, and they had come from summery Virginia with few clothes or blankets and with no wagon transport. But Major General Carter L. Stevenson, commanding at Sweetwater, had no surplus supplies to offer. And to add to Longstreet's woes, at this point Bragg began to berate him for falling behind schedule.

"Thus," wrote Longstreet after the War, his anger still barely suppressed, "we found ourselves in a strange country, not as much as a day's rations on hand, with hardly enough land transportation for ordinary camp equipage, the enemy in front to be captured, and our friends in rear putting in their paper bullets." It was beginning to look, he said, "more like a campaign against Longstreet than against Burnside."

Longstreet persevered as best he could and led his men northward. But he had little heart for the coming confrontation with an adversary he had faced 11 months before, on the bloody hills of Fredericksburg.

Ambrose Burnside had failed conspicuously at Fredericksburg and had lost his command and his reputation because of it. But he had accepted the blame and had soldiered on, determined to serve his country and restore his good name. He had served both those causes well in his advance on Knoxville.

Burnside left Cincinnati in mid-August with the three divisions of his Army of the Ohio. The logical route to Knoxville led through the Confederate-held Cumberland Gap, a position that strongly favored the defenders. Rather than risk heavy losses in a pitched battle for the gap, Burnside chose to flank the Confederates out of their position.

He sent one division, commanded by Colonel John F. DeCourcy, to threaten the gap from the north. Then Burnside took his other two divisions into the rugged mountains of East Tennessee on routes toward Knoxville that would take them 40 miles to the south of the Confederate position.

To speed his marching columns through the formidable terrain, Burnside used pack mules instead of supply wagons. But the roads were so steep that horses drawing the artillery often were stopped in their tracks; when that happened, an observer reported, "the worn and struggling animals gave place to men who, with hands and shoulders to the wheels and limber, hoisted guns and caissons from height to height." The roadside was littered with the wreckage of caissons and the bodies of exhausted draft animals. A number of pack mules slipped on the precipitous trails and tumbled to their death; in some instances their drivers went with them. "If this is the kind of country we are fighting for, I am in favor of letting the Rebs take their land," wrote an enlisted man, J. W. Gaskill of the 104th Ohio.

Despite the difficulties, the men made remarkable progress—marching as much as 30 miles a day. Although they did not know it en route, they were being blessed with good fortune. Most of the Confederates in the area had been withdrawn southward to reinforce Bragg at Chattanooga. Only one brigade remained in Cumberland Gap and another east of Knoxville.

After fretting for weeks over the size and

On their way west after the Fredericksburg Campaign in February 1863, men of the Federal IX Corps wait to board transports at Aquia Creek Landing, Virginia. Eventually they joined Burnside's Army of the Ohio near Lexington, Kentucky.

safety of his attacking force, Burnside approached Knoxville in early September virtually unopposed. More than that, he was wildly welcomed.

Most East Tennesseans had shown strong support for the Union from the outbreak of the War. In the balloting over secession in 1861, they had voted 2 to 1 to remain in the Union—and it was said that the margin would have been around 5 to 1, save for the fact that many Unionists had been intimidated and thousands of Confederate soldiers had cast illegal ballots. In the two years since, these antisecession Southerners had known civil war at its rawest. They were imprisoned by the hundreds as traitors and had otherwise suffered grievously at the hands of the Confederates.

A petition from the Unionists was presented to the Federal Congress in 1864 seeking redress; the document was a litany of abuses and persecutions. Property, the petition said, "has been seized, confiscated; their houses pillaged; their stock driven off; their grain consumed; their substance wasted; their fences burned; their fields laid waste; their farms destroyed."

Depredations upon human beings had been even worse. Unionist Tennesseans, the document stated, "have been beaten with ropes, with straps and with clubs. Some have been butchered, others shot down in their own homes or yards—in the highroad, or the fields, or in the forests." The petition concluded grimly: "There is no single neighborhood within the bounds of East Tennessee whose green sod has not drunk the blood of citizens murdered."

Under the circumstances, it was not surprising that the advancing Federal troops were greeted as deliverers, with a fervor that

few of the soldiers ever forgot. As the men approached Knoxville, crowds stood by the sides of the roads shouting out their thanks and admiration. "H'ain't they purty!" cried a party of mountain girls. "At every house," one soldier recalled, "the entire family would appear, often with buckets of fresh water and fruit for the welcome Yankees. Old gray-haired men would come out and seize the General's hand, bidding him Godspeed, and men would flock in at every halt to be armed and join us."

A brigade of Burnside's cavalry entered Knoxville on September 2, and the general arrived with his main force the next day—to a tumultuous welcome. At Burnside's new headquarters a soldier unfurled the garrison flag and hung it from a balcony; the crowd went mad. "Shout after shout rent the air," recalled the soldier. "Old men and gray-haired matrons took each other by the hand and laughed, shook and cried, all at the same time. Young men and maidens were uproarious, and little children were 'clean gone crazy.'" Inside the headquarters building, Burnside and two of his generals had been caught up in the emotion: The three officers were shaking hands, while tears ran down their cheeks. It was, said more than one witness, like the Fourth of July.

The arrival had been spectacular, but Burnside could not spend much time savoring it. The Confederates still held Cumberland Gap, and now came word that Colonel DeCourcy had halted at the northern approach, convinced that his force was too small to break through. Burnside immediately sent a brigade of cavalry under Brigadier General James M. Shackelford to advance against the gap from the south.

The hard-pressed Confederates had entrusted Cumberland Gap to a totally inadequate force of 2,300 inexperienced soldiers commanded by Brigadier General John W. Frazer. It was originally assumed that Frazer could ward off an attacking force until he could be reinforced from Knoxville. Ordered to hold the position at all costs, Frazer had diligently set about building defense works against an attack from the north, and he had expressed confidence that he could resist a siege for at least a month.

But then the Confederates in Knoxville were ordered to pull out for Chattanooga as Burnside approached — and no one made it clear to Frazer what he was supposed to do. On September 7 the dismayed Confederate was confronted by General Shackelford, who had arrived from Knoxville, demanding his surrender. Frazer refused, only to encounter the same demand the next day by DeCourcy — who apparently had been prodded into action by Shackelford's arrival at the opposite end of the gap. The plucky Frazer, though bottled up in the gap, refused again to surrender.

At that point Burnside left Knoxville for the gap with an infantry brigade commanded by Colonel Samuel A. Gilbert. Always a swift marcher, Burnside brought this unit over the 60-mile distance in only 52 hours. Suddenly Frazer found himself facing a new surrender demand, now from an overwhelming force commanded by Burnside himself. On September 9 Frazer capitulated.

Having won Knoxville so handily, Burnside answered General Rosecrans' request for some cavalry and made preparations to move eastward to seize Confederate salt works in Virginia. Then, as the confrontation at Chickamauga loomed, officials in Washington tried in vain to get Burnside to go south to reinforce Rosecrans in strength. "These instructions were repeated some fifteen times," Halleck told Grant later, "but were not carried out." Burnside stubbornly insisted on holding the territory that he had won and protecting the Unionists there.

After Chickamauga, Burnside was ordered to move closer to Rosecrans' trapped army in Chattanooga. But still Burnside seemed to feel no urgency. The day after the battle at Chickamauga he sent President Lincoln a business-as-usual dispatch that finally shattered the President's patience.

On September 25 Lincoln penned a scathing reply. Burnside's message, he wrote, "makes me doubt whether I am awake or dreaming. I have been struggling for ten days, first through General Halleck, and then directly, to get you to go to assist General Rosecrans in an extremity, and you have repeatedly declared you would do it, and yet you steadily move the contrary way." There was more in the same vein. Then, when the President had committed his fury to paper, he folded the letter, wrote on it "Not sent" and stuffed it in his pocket. Burnside never saw it. Instead he received a more temperate reply, suggesting that he hold Knoxville with some of his men and send Rosecrans the rest. He must not worry about Knoxville's fate. "East Tennessee," said Lincoln, "can be no more than temporarily lost so long as Chattanooga is firmly held."

The fact is, the President himself was no longer quite so sure of the advisability of moving Burnside from Knoxville. For one thing, the Army of the Ohio was encountering supply problems almost as severe as those afflicting the Army of the Cumberland. The single wagon road through Cumberland Gap was proving inadequate to keep

Major General Ambrose E. Burnside embarked on the campaign in eastern Tennessee determined to redeem the reputation he had lost at Fredericksburg. He was confident of success, he wrote General Grant, and "ready to meet any force the enemy might send against us."

Burnside's men in food, ammunition and other necessities. If Burnside moved even farther from his already strained supply line, he might find himself in serious trouble.

Moreover, the inactivity around Chattanooga in the weeks following Chickamauga perhaps indicated a Confederate change of plan. Bragg did not seem to be preparing an

attack, Lincoln observed to Rosecrans early in October; it now appeared much more likely that the Confederates would try "a concentrated drive at Burnside." As was often the case, the President's observation was prescient: Shortly before Lincoln had written these words, Jefferson Davis arrived at Bragg's headquarters, and soon thereafter he conceived the idea of sending Longstreet to attack Burnside.

As Longstreet started toward Knoxville on November 5, the Lincoln Administration, having tried for weeks to get Burnside to abandon the place, now became determined to hold the town; and the Federal high command also grew deeply concerned about Burnside's welfare. General Grant wrote that his superiors "plied me with dispatches faster than ever, urging that something should be done for his relief." Grant indeed tried something: He called on General George Thomas to mount an attack on Bragg's lines at Chattanooga, in the hope that it would cause Bragg to recall Longstreet. But Grant was told that the attack was impossible — there were not enough healthy horses left in Chattanooga to pull Thomas' artillery.

Grant could only encourage Burnside to hold fast until some way could be found to send him help. But Burnside responded with calm confidence. The Army of the Ohio was in no trouble, he assured Grant, and could hold out as long as its ammunition lasted. In fact, Burnside thought he might be able to help Grant: By meeting Longstreet south of Knoxville, engaging the Confederates and giving ground slowly, he could protract the affair and keep Longstreet out of the forthcoming battle at Chattanooga. Grant was delighted and instantly accepted the suggestion. Burnside left a strong force behind to bolster the Knoxville defenses and set out with about 5,000 troops to meet Longstreet.

On November 13, as the ragged Confederates toiled northward along the railroad line, Longstreet sent three brigades of Wheeler's cavalry ahead on a dash to Knoxville. Wheeler's mission was to occupy the commanding heights on the south bank of the Holston River across from the town. But when his horsemen neared Knoxville on the 15th, they found their path blocked by two regiments of Burnside's cavalry under Brigadier General William P. Sanders, an officer highly respected for his skill and energy. Although his troopers were outnumbered and less experienced than those of Wheeler, Sanders was able to slow the Confederate approach to a crawl. And when Wheeler finally pushed his way to the heights south of the town, he found them heavily fortified and unassailable. There was nothing to do but rejoin Longstreet's main force.

On November 15, meanwhile, as the Con-

Mules for Burnside's invasion of East Tennessee were kept in split-rail pens at Camp Nelson near Lexington, Kentucky. Burnside's liberal use of pack mules during the invasion was in the tradition of the frontier armies in which he had served before the War.

Standing in a litter of horseshoes, four farriers at Camp Nelson pause while shoeing a mule suspended in a sling. The mule's head is clamped securely, and its hoofs are immobilized by restraining straps, one of which can be seen binding the animal's right rear fetlock.

federate infantrymen were in the process of crossing the Tennessee River 30 miles south of Knoxville, Longstreet received a startling report: His enemy was on the other side of the river, just five miles to the east, and evidently withdrawing before the Confederates. Longstreet smelled a victory. He had all but outflanked the Federals. If he reached Lenoir's Station, about eight miles to the northeast, before Burnside arrived there, he could cut the Federals' line of retreat and destroy them. But Burnside was moving too

fast. By the time the Confederate troops reached Lenoir's Station on November 16, the Federals had pulled out.

Before long, however, the Confederates got another opportunity to cut Burnside off. The approaches to Knoxville narrowed to a single road at Campbell's Station, a crossroads about 15 miles southwest of Knoxville. At 2 a.m. on the 16th, while Burnside's troops, led by his wagon trains, were withdrawing to Campbell's Station through a downpour, a Southern sympathizer showed

Longstreet a route to the crossroads that was shorter and undefended by the Federals. Longstreet immediately sent McLaws driving down this road, with cavalry in the lead, in another effort to get between Burnside and Knoxville. At the same time, Jenkins' division pressed Burnside's rear guard.

As McLaws' men hurried along, they happened to brush the Federal right flank. Burnside, now alerted to the danger, sped Brigadier General John F. Hartranft's division toward Campbell's Station.

It was a deadly race — in the mud. Private William Todd of the 79th New York High-landers recalled that between 5 a.m. and day-break on November 16 the Federal wagons covered only two miles in heavy muck. "It was dark and disagreeable," he said; "the mud was deep and the road full of wagons and artillery, which we were frequently obliged to help out of the mud holes." At last, orders were issued to abandon scores of the wagons — to the great pleasure of Long-street's hungry, ill-clad, poorly equipped soldiers who came along behind.

The vanguards of both forces were rushing through the mired roads toward Campbell's Station. For a time, the outcome was

Bending into a driving rainstorm, men of Burnside's army strain at the wheels of cannon and limbers to get their artillery up a mountain road during the campaign in eastern Tennessee. "Wagons sank to their boxes in the liquid mud," wrote a correspondent on the scene, "while drivers, teamsters and artillerymen became so covered with the spattering mud that it was difficult to tell them from the surrounding soil."

uncertain. The Federal soldiers arrived first, around noon, but only by about a quarter of an hour; Hartranft had scarcely positioned his troops to cover the crossroads when they came under fire from McLaws' men.

Longstreet had learned from intelligence reports that he outnumbered the Federals and he had little doubt that he could drive them from Campbell's Station — but to send Burnside reeling back into the safety of the Knoxville defenses would serve no purpose. On the other hand, Longstreet noted, "as the enemy stood he was ours." If Longstreet could flank the Federals, he might still get between them and Knoxville and destroy them at his leisure.

Accordingly, Longstreet ordered Jenkins to send two brigades from his division on a sweep wide to the right. These brigades, under the command of Brigadier General Evander Law, would knife between Burnside and Knoxville and fall on the Federal rear. To distract Burnside while Law was getting into position, General McLaws was ordered to attack the Federal right and pin down the enemy forces there.

The muddle that now ensued became the subject of much dispute after the War. A bitter professional rivalry between Jenkins and Law had been festering for some time, and this ill will may have contributed to the controversy. McLaws carried out his assignment — his attack forced the troops of Burnside's right to fall back — but the rest of the Confederate movement misfired. A few minutes after McLaws launched his attack, Jenkins wrote in his official account, "greatly to my surprise, I received a message from General Law that in advancing his brigade had obliqued so much to the left as to have gotten out of its line of attack." Law's men may

have been confused by the terrain; at any rate, by the time they could be redirected, Burnside, having watched the Confederate movement from a nearby hill, had moved to defend his rear. By nightfall the Confederate opportunity had passed. Law's "causeless and inexcusable movement," charged Jenkins, "lost us the few moments in which success from this point could be attained."

The engagement at Campbell's Station ended in frustration for the Confederates. The Federals held the crossroads that night until most of their wagons were safely past, then they followed the trains into the town before dawn. In the meantime, there was a brisk, if not very damaging, exchange of artillery fire. "This has been called a battle by the other side," Longstreet later observed dryly, "but it was only an artillery combat, little, very little, musket ammunition being burnt." Federal losses were about 300, including 31 killed; Confederate casualties amounted to 22 dead and 152 wounded.

Still, Burnside had cause for satisfaction. The withdrawal to Knoxville under Confederate pressure had been well executed, and had delayed Longstreet — reputed to be one of the South's best generals — for almost a week. By November 17 Burnside's army was safely within the Knoxville defenses.

General Sanders' cavalry had been deployed to cover the last leg of Burnside's retreat. Sanders successfully held Longstreet at bay — but at a great cost. On November 18 Sanders was killed in a skirmish. He had bought time for Burnside's troops to complete their fortifications. "Every day of delay added to the strength of the enemy's breastworks," wrote Longstreet's artillery commander, Colonel Edward Porter Alexander. In a few days the Federals had a sec-

ond defensive line inside the first. Hoping to receive additional troops from Bragg or from western Virginia, Longstreet waited and examined the ground.

Knoxville was situated on the north bank of the Holston River, a major tributary of the Tennessee. The formidable Federal defenses formed three sides of a rectangle enclosing the town against the river. On the west the Confederates would face a short line that ran north to a substantial fort. There the line turned eastward and extended across the back of the town; here the guns and muskets covered open fields, flooded by two creeks that flowed through the town into the Holston. The Federal line then turned south, to link up again with the river.

It was apparent from the beginning, according to Colonel Alexander, that the most imposing feature of the Federal defenses—

Two images are joined to produce this panoramic view east toward downtown Knoxville during the siege. Federal earthworks line the hills in the far distance and also the southern heights across the Tennessee River at far right. The Confederate attack came from the northwest, behind and to the left of where the photographer was standing. Union cannon can be seen in the right foreground.

the fort at the northwest corner — was also its weakest link. The redoubt had been named Fort Sanders in honor of Burnside's slain cavalry chief. It had thick earthen walls eight feet high and was fronted by a 12-foot-wide ditch — the depth of which was about to become a critical factor. Cannon emplaced in bastions projecting from the corners of the fort completely enfiladed the ditch in front. But the fort had a significant flaw — it was situated only 120 yards from a broad creekbed in which large numbers of troops could assemble completely under cover. All things considered, said Alexander, it was the "one point of the lines which it was possible to assault with any hope of success." But Longstreet seemed to be in no hurry.

The waiting was hard on both armies. Burnside had built a pontoon bridge across the Holston to collect supplies from the south side of the river, where his cavalry continued to hold the high ground. Still, food and forage were scarce in Knoxville. Despite the efforts of sympathetic residents of the area, the Federals soon were on reduced rations, subsisting on a slender daily issue of salt pork and a bread that had more roughage than nutrition. Many draft animals were slain so they would not have to be fed, and their carcasses were thrown in the river.

The Confederate besiegers were, if anything, in more desperate straits than the besieged: They were a long way from their nearest base, and they were among unfriendly people. Moreover, Longstreet's divisions had not been well supplied to begin with.

Besides food and forage, the Confederates badly needed shoes for both men and horses. Colonel Alexander wrote that he saw "bloody stains on frozen ground, left by the

barefooted where our infantry had passed."
With Longstreet's concurrence, his troops
appropriated footwear from captured Federals. (One prisoner accepted the situation
philosophically: "When a man is captured,"
he reasoned, "his shoes are captured, too.")
After Burnside's Federals began to slaughter
draft animals and dump them in the river,
the Confederates downstream fished out the
carcasses and stripped them of their shoes.

As time passed, Longstreet pondered a
plan of attack. The situation called for a
straightforward assault: Alexander's artillery would bombard the fort and soften up
the defenses, sharpshooters would take the
rifle pits outside the walls, and finally the
infantry would charge. Four of Alexander's
howitzers were put on skids to give them a
lofty trajectory; they could then be used as
mortars to lob shells over the fort's walls. In
addition, 30 other guns were aimed at the
little fort. All was ready by November 24.

But that night Longstreet learned that
reinforcements—two brigades, 2,600 men,
under Brigadier Generals Bushrod Johnson
and Archibald Gracie Jr.—were on their
way from Bragg, and Longstreet decided to
wait for them. Then on the evening of the
25th there arrived Bragg's chief engineer,
Brigadier General Danville Leadbetter—
the man who had laid out Knoxville's defenses when it was in Confederate hands. He
encouraged Longstreet to consider attacking
the other end of the town, an idea that
proved utterly impractical and further delayed the attack.

On the 26th, after a fruitless reconnaissance with Leadbetter, Longstreet was scanning the enemy fort through his field glasses
when he noticed a Federal soldier walking
across the ditch in front of Fort Sanders. Un-

aware that a plank was used for this purpose,
Longstreet concluded happily that the ditch
was shallow enough to be crossed without
undue difficulty. Nor did the steep earthen
walls seem to present an acute problem: Jenkins had proposed that if the attackers did
have trouble scaling the walls, they could dig
footholds in them.

The assault was rescheduled for noon on
November 28; but it rained all day, and
Longstreet ordered another delay. By this
time Longstreet and his men were hearing
rumors of a Federal victory at Chattanooga.
The reports, though unconfirmed, prompted McLaws on the evening of the 28th to
urge Longstreet to end the siege of Knoxville

…r the attack on Fort Sanders, Con-
…derate General James Longstreet
…ose Georgia and Mississippi veter-
…s who had served him well in the
…st. Despite his reservations
…out the campaign, he insisted
… the eve of attack that he had "no
…prehension of the result if we go at
…with determination."

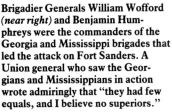

Brigadier Generals William Wofford (*near right*) and Benjamin Humphreys were the commanders of the Georgia and Mississippi brigades that led the attack on Fort Sanders. A Union general who saw the Georgians and Mississippians in action wrote admiringly that "they had few equals, and I believe no superiors."

and retreat to Virginia; if Bragg had indeed been defeated the whole Federal army would surely be turned on Longstreet. Perhaps so, said Longstreet. He was no admirer of Bragg's. But if he now retreated, Longstreet reasoned, a defeated Bragg would be left "at the mercy of his victors." They must attack, said Longstreet: "There is neither safety nor honor in any other course."

But late that night Longstreet made a sudden and inexplicable change that dismayed Alexander. The infantry attack would be launched at dawn, without benefit of the carefully prepared artillery barrage. Apparently Longstreet thought surprise would be of greater benefit than the cannonade. Yet he lost the element of surprise by ordering the skirmishers to take the outlying Federal rifle pits immediately after moonrise.

At 11 p.m. the Confederate skirmishers advanced. Sharp fighting continued for two hours; when it was over, about 50 of the Federal soldiers had been taken prisoner, and the rest had been driven back into their own lines. The action, strange as it was, did indeed improve the Confederate position and place sharpshooters within range of the Federal defenders on the walls of the fort. But it was also a clear signal of the impending attack. When the Confederates charged the fort a few hours later, the Federals who would bear the brunt of the attack — the 79th New York — were waiting for them.

Longstreet intended to take the fort by a bayonet charge. He assigned the attack to McLaws' three brigades and instructed one of Jenkins' brigades to provide support on the left. Then he issued orders that no one fire except the sharpshooters in the newly captured rifle pits — and they were to "pick off every head that might appear above the parapets until the fort was carried." So carefully was this order observed, said Captain D. Augustus Dickert, that "not a gun was loaded in three brigades."

It was a morning made raw by rain and snow, and the ground was frozen and rime-covered. The attackers waded through the waist-deep creek whose banks hid them from the defenders. "Shivering in their wet garments," said Dickert, the Confederates awaited the signal to advance. They were about 120 yards from the fort. A few rounds from signal guns launched the charge.

As the Confederates ran forward yelling, the Federal guns and muskets opened fire at point-blank range. The attackers were coming from such a short distance that "there was no need to take aim," a Federal soldier noted. The Confederates, wrote a Northern correspondent, were "stunned for a moment by the torrent of canister and lead poured upon them," but they never hesitated.

Suddenly the leaders of the charge began falling to the ground and cursing. The Federals had strung telegraph wire knee-high among the stumps left when the approaches to the fort were cleared; it was perhaps the first use of wire entanglements during the War. Cries of "Halt!" came from the Confederate officers, but the men could not stop. Pressed on from behind, they stumbled; more men pushed forward, the journalist noted, "and fell amid the dead and dying."

The wires were quickly cleared away, and the line of attackers leaped into the ditch. As it turned out, the ditch was on the average eight feet deep; once in it the men were confronted by an almost vertical, ice-covered

In this view of the assault on Fort Sanders, attacking Confederate troops attempt to charge up a slope toward the fort's northwestern bastion but find themselves entangled in a web of telegraph wire strung among tree stumps. In the background, attackers under enfilading fire try to climb out of the deep ditch before the fort and scale the earthen walls.

wall rising 16 feet before them. They were trapped. A murderous fire poured down on the attackers, and men fell by the scores. There was no way anyone could have dug footholds in the wall under that fire. Some soldiers leaped onto the shoulders of their comrades and tried to reach the top of the wall. Those who made it were instantly shot down. Lieutenant Samuel L. Benjamin, the Federal artillery commander in the fort, had instructed his men to prepare 50 cannon shells with three-second fuses. Now the defenders lit the fuses and tossed the shells over the parapet among the attackers. "It stilled them down," said Benjamin grimly.

It was a massacre. "The earth," wrote the Northern correspondent, "was sated in blood — men waded in blood, and struggled up the scarp, and slipping in blood fell back to join their mangled predecessors in the gory mud below. The shouts of the foiled and infuriate Rebels, the groans of the dying and shrieks of the wounded arose above the din of the cannon."

A few attackers got to the top long enough to plant their battle flags. One young officer, Adjutant T. W. Cumming of the 16th Georgia, climbed through an embrasure and was immediately dragged inside. He endeared himself to his captors by demanding their surrender before he was marched away.

For a while Confederate soldiers continued to mill helplessly in the ditch and at the base of the wall, unable to advance and unwilling to retreat through the furious Federal fire that was raking the open fields. Finally some began to slip away. Others surrendered. Inside the fort, one weary Irish prisoner took out his pipe, reached for a light and said wryly to his captured mates: "Bedad, boys, General Longstreet said we would be

in Knoxville for breakfast this morning; and so some of us are!"

After about 20 minutes of fighting, Longstreet approached to within 500 yards of the fort and observed a disaster in the making. As he later reported: "I saw some of the men straggling back, and heard that the troops could not pass the ditch for want of ladders or other means. Almost at the same moment I saw that the men were beginning to retire in considerable numbers, and very soon the column broke up entirely and fell back in confusion." The Confederate commander called a halt to the slaughter. By the time the firing died down, his men had suffered heavy losses — 813 casualties in those few bloody minutes — and had done little damage to the enemy. Burnside's casualties in the fort totaled eight dead and five wounded. It was "Fredericksburg reversed," said Captain Henry Burrage of the 36th Massachusetts, who had served in Virginia.

The field in front of the fort was littered with dead and wounded, and immediately after the battle Burnside offered Longstreet a truce so he could gather up his casualties. Longstreet gratefully accepted.

Then the Confederate general pulled his

Among the tree stumps that stand in the path of Confederate assault columns, Captain Orlando Poe *(near right)*, builder of Union defensive works at Fort Sanders, confers with Lieutenant Colonel Orville Babcock, Burnside's senior engineer. In the far distance, a lone sentry stands atop the fort's northwest bastion, which took the brunt of the Confederate attack. The same bastion, along with the fort's main defense ditch, appears in the close-up view below, taken shortly after the siege.

forces together and began to assess his situation. But just half an hour after the repulse a courier brought a message from President Davis about Chattanooga. Momentous events had occurred there, and they would alter Longstreet's plans completely.

Ulysses S. Grant was an offensive-minded soldier, and he had found it intolerable to be cooped up in Chattanooga, surrounded by towering hills and trapped by a threatening enemy. "I have never felt such restlessness before," he wrote, "as I have at the fixed and immovable condition of the Army of the Cumberland."

To defeat the Confederates and retain the town, Grant would have to attack an enemy entrenched on high ground, and he planned his offensive carefully. Grant had three forces at his disposal; he elected to give the pivotal role in the assault to the Army of the Tennessee, commanded by his old friend, General Sherman. There were few men in the world Grant trusted as he did Sherman — and he had faith in Sherman's army, for it was his own former command.

Grant viewed the other two forces with less enthusiasm. He suspected that General Joseph Hooker and his XI and XII Corps had been sent to him as the castoffs of the Army of the Potomac. His third force, the Army of the Cumberland, had been through a crushing defeat, and he was worried about the soldiers' state of mind. According to Sherman, Grant thought that the men of Thomas' army "had been so demoralized by the battle of Chickamauga that he feared they could not be got out of their trenches to assume the offensive."

To make best use of Sherman and his army, Grant had contrived an artful plan.

The target would be the Confederate right — at the junction of Bragg's supply line from the south and his line of communication with Longstreet to the north. Sherman was to march upriver from Bridgeport to Brown's Ferry, cross to the north side of the Tennessee and move into the hills north of Chattanooga. This movement could not be hidden from the watchful Confederates on Lookout Mountain, but Grant hoped to confuse them about where the Federals were going.

As Sherman's Army of the Tennessee neared Lookout Mountain, one division was to be detached for a feint against Bragg's left. The rest of Sherman's army would disappear from Confederate view marching northward — as if to Knoxville. But once safely out of sight on the north side of the river, the men would make camp and lie hidden. Then, in a rapid nighttime move, Sherman was to bridge the river — General William Smith was already hard at work making the necessary pontoons — whisk his men across and, before Bragg knew what was happening, roll up the Confederate right flank along Missionary Ridge. Bragg would thus be cut off from his supply base at Chickamauga Station and driven away, if not destroyed.

Hooker and Thomas were to play supporting roles. Grant had first planned to have Hooker's XII Corps attack Lookout Mountain, but he decided that this would not be necessary — the height would lose its importance if Sherman took Missionary Ridge. Grant instead assigned Hooker's troops to move around Lookout Mountain and threaten the Confederate left at Rossville Gap. Major General Oliver O. Howard was to place XI Corps in reserve on the north side of the Tennessee River, across from Chattanooga. Thomas was to give artillery support to Sherman and later to assault the enemy center.

On November 16 Grant took Sherman to view the field and pointed out the objective for the Army of the Tennessee. Sherman stared through a telescope at the left end of Missionary Ridge, then closed up the glass with an audible snap and said: "I can do it!"

The attack was scheduled for daylight on the 21st. Sherman hurried back to Bridgeport and on the 17th had his lead units on the road for the 27-mile march. But then the elements began to conspire against him. As Sherman's footsore soldiers headed for Chattanooga, rain began to fall and the roads turned to mud, slowing the march to a crawl. It was November 20 before the vanguard of Sherman's three divisions reached the pontoon bridge at Brown's Ferry. The rest of his army was strung all the way back to Bridgeport. It was impossible to make the deadline; only one of Sherman's divisions could be brought into line by the 21st, and the others would not even be across the bridge at Brown's Ferry. Grant reluctantly yielded to reality, but he pressed Sherman: "Can you not get up for the following morning?"

Sherman tried. He urged his troops forward in a fresh downpour that began on the 20th and continued through the 21st. The roads grew much worse, and the river began to rise, threatening the pontoon bridge. When all of Sherman's divisions but one were across, the bridge finally gave way — stranding the remaining men, commanded by Brigadier General Peter J. Osterhaus. Grant quickly ordered Osterhaus to join Hooker's troops in Lookout Valley, and Sherman's other divisions disappeared into the hills above Chattanooga.

Soon after the Army of the Tennessee was safely hidden from the Confederates, Howard's XI Corps, in the same hills, emerged within their enemy's sight, crossed the bridge at Chattanooga and moved behind Thomas' defenses. This put the finishing touch to Grant's ruse. He hoped that the Confederates, having seen soldiers crossing at Brown's Ferry and, a short time later, seeing soldiers moving across the river into Chattanooga, would conclude that they were the same soldiers. To make up for the loss of Osterhaus, Grant assigned Sherman one of Thomas' divisions, commanded by Brigadier General Jefferson C. Davis.

Much time had been lost — it was now November 22 — but Grant was just about ready. Sherman's advance was rescheduled for November 24.

As Grant had hoped, the Confederates were thoroughly confused. Bragg, watching all those enemy troops moving around, fretted about Sherman's location. Was the Army of the Tennessee preparing for a flanking attack on Lookout Mountain? Was it headed toward Knoxville? Or had Sherman merely reinforced Thomas in Chattanooga? Bragg finally concluded that Sherman was marching on Knoxville, and on November 22 he ordered Simon Buckner's and Patrick Cleburne's divisions to entrain for the north to reinforce Longstreet. Buckner left immediately. Cleburne marched his troops to the railroad yards and awaited the return of the train carrying Buckner and his men.

Bragg was deeply worried about the fate of Knoxville. Two days previously, he had made an attempt to immobilize Grant and prevent him from strengthening Burnside any further. He had decided to employ a subterfuge of his own, sending Grant a curious communication under a flag of truce. "As there may still be some noncombatants in

The Stalwart Scots of Fort Sanders

The Federal troops who had the lion's share of fighting at Fort Sanders were the 79th New York Highlanders, a regiment comprising mostly Scottish-born immigrants. Wearing kilts or tartan pants called trews, the Highlanders had marched to war in 1861 while their pipes and drums played "The Campbells Are Coming," a rousing Scottish air.

By 1863, the Highlanders had fought from Bull Run to Antietam to Vicksburg. Their kilts and trews had given way to uniforms of standard blue, and only the soft forage caps, called Glengarries — and the burr in their speech — identified the men's origins. The 79th reached Knoxville on November 17 and worked feverishly to build up the earthen fort, cutting embrasures in its walls and placing bales of cotton atop the low parapets. When the Confederates finally charged on November 29, they piled into the ditch in front of the fort and were annihilated by the Highlanders' fire. A Scotsman wrote: "Almost every bullet fired by us found a death mark."

The Highlanders lost only four men. They were buried in a military cemetery alongside other Highlanders who died during the campaign, and stonecutters in the ranks carved memorials (below, foreground) to the men they left behind.

HIGHLANDER JAMES BERRY IN GLENGARRY CAP

Headstones and a small monument (center) carved by New York Highlanders mark the graves of comrades who fell during the Knoxville Campaign.

Chattanooga," Bragg wrote, " I deem it proper to notify you that prudence would dictate their early withdrawal."

Grant had puzzled over this message. That it was a heavy-handed attempt at deception was evident; for some reason Bragg wanted Grant to think he was planning an attack. But why? The mystery deepened on November 22, when a Confederate deserter came to the Federals with a report that Bragg was pulling back from Missionary Ridge.

The report was, of course, false. The deserter may have misinterpreted Buckner's departure that day as a general withdrawal. In any case, the report galvanized Grant. He urgently needed to know whether the Confederates were actually withdrawing. If so, this would be an ideal moment to strike them. Someone must test the Rebel reflexes. Sherman was not ready; but Thomas was.

Early on the morning of November 23 Grant gave Thomas his instructions. In Chattanooga Valley, the plain lying between the town and Missionary Ridge to the east, there was a wooded mound called Orchard Knob. For weeks, Confederate troops had held the valley, including the hillock; their entrenchments in the cotton fields, according to a Federal officer, gave the place the appearance of a prairie-dog village. Thomas was to conduct a reconnaissance in force toward Orchard Knob to see if the Confederate positions in the valley were still occupied. At his discretion, he could seize Orchard Knob.

As Thomas was fully aware, the entire operation would be closely watched by friend and foe alike. The Chattanooga Valley and its surrounding hills formed a magnificent amphitheater; both the Confederates on their eminences and the Federals camped along the river bluffs of the town could clearly see all that occurred on the plain between them. Grant wrote later that it was "the first battle field I have ever seen where a plan could be followed, and from one place the whole field be within one view."

Onto this stage at noon on November 23 marched the division of Brigadier General Thomas J. Wood, whose shift of position on the field of Chickamauga two months before had brought disaster to the Army of the Cumberland. On Wood's right marched Major General Philip Sheridan's division, which had also fled before Longstreet's onslaught on that September day. The men of Thomas' army were still smarting over the memory of the rout — and over Grant's scarcely concealed suspicion that the experience had ruined them as a fighting force. They were eager to prove him wrong. Brigadier General Absalom Baird's division would lend support on the Federal right, and Howard's corps was in reserve on the left.

As the troops marched briskly out of the Chattanooga defenses, Grant watched from one of the nearby hills, surrounded by high-ranking officers. "It was an inspiring sight," wrote Lieutenant Colonel Joseph S. Fullerton, "Flags were flying; the quick, earnest steps of thousands beat equal time. The sharp commands of hundreds of company officers, the sound of the drums, the ringing notes of the bugle, companies wheeling and countermarching and regiments getting into line, the bright sun lighting up ten thousand polished bayonets till they glistened and flashed like a flying shower of electric sparks — all looked like preparations for a peaceful pageant, rather than for the bloody work of death."

Men everywhere stopped to watch. On the hills looming over the plain, clusters of Confederates could be seen staring at the display. Like many of the Federals, they believed for a moment that Thomas was staging a grand review. Then a signal cannon boomed, and Thomas' lines started forward, "moving," continued Fullerton, "with the steadiness of a machine." Drummers marched beside the advancing troops, beating the charge. Charles Dana, standing next to Grant, was awestruck. "The spectacle," he said, "was one of singular magnificence."

Suddenly the Confederates realized they were under attack and scurried for cover. The Confederate pickets fell back to the lines that had been established before Orchard Knob. "Firing opened from the enemy's advanced rifle pits," Lieutenant Colonel Fullerton wrote, "followed by a tremendous roll of musketry and roar of artillery." After a time, recalled Fullerton, "men were seen on the ground, dotting the field over which the line of battle had passed. Ambulances came hurrying back with the first of the wounded. Columns of puffy smoke arose from the Orchard Knob woods."

The watchers in Chattanooga heard a faint cheer from the Knob. And all at once it was over. "The entire movement was carried out in such an incredibly short time," said Dana, "that at half past three I was able to send a telegram to Stanton describing the victory."

For a victory it had been. Instead of simply driving in Bragg's pickets, the Federals had seized the ground. "You have gained too much to withdraw," Thomas said in a message to Wood. "Hold your position and I will support you." For Grant, the extension of his lines toward the Confederate center was unexpected but welcome. "This movement," he said, "secured to us a line fully a mile in advance of the one we occupied in the

morning." On his orders the captured Confederate fortifications were revised so that they faced the Confederates, and that night the works were strengthened.

It had been a minor action, but one with noteworthy results. The skirmish made it abundantly clear to Grant that Bragg was still on the scene, but the fight also served to rouse the Confederate commander from his apathy. There was no mistaking that Grant was in a mood to act. Hastily, Bragg recalled Cleburne's division from Chickamauga Station, where it was just about to board the train to Knoxville, and put it back in the line around Chattanooga; it was to play a critical role in the coming battle. Then Bragg pulled a division off Lookout Mountain and placed it in the Missionary Ridge defenses.

In the game of cat-and-mouse that Grant and Bragg had been playing, Grant had seized the advantage, and he intended to keep it. Sherman's men by now were all in position, hidden in the woods eight miles northeast of Chattanooga. Few of them knew what their role was to be; the secrecy cloaking Sherman's plans was so tight that civilians in the area of his encampment were placed under guard to keep any word from leaking out. In North Chickamauga Creek, which led into the Tennessee River, 116 pontoons lay hidden and waiting.

On November 24 just before midnight, 30 Federal scouts quietly rowed across the river to the south bank. They walked boldly up to the Confederate pickets from behind, announced themselves as the relief and captured the sentries without firing a shot. While the scouts secured the landing, one brigade of Sherman's soldiers slipped down to the water's edge on the north bank and waited for the boats. At 2 a.m. General

William Tecumseh Sherman, whom a fellow officer once called "the concentrated quintessence of Yankeedom," was Grant's most trusted general and one of the Union's ablest commanders. "All his features express determination," the officer continued, "particularly the mouth."

Smith's pontoons noiselessly grounded on the north shore; their passage down the river from their hiding place had been so quiet that even the Federal pickets had been unaware of the boats' approach.

The troops began to board. As Captain Samuel H. M. Byers of the 5th Iowa headed for his craft, he heard a low voice from the bank: "Be prompt as you can, boys, there's room for thirty in a boat," and he peered at a tall figure standing in the darkness. It was Sherman. His presence, said Byers, "waked confidence in everyone. He was with us, and sharing the danger."

The pontoons began ferrying men across, and work started on a bridge. As each boat returned from ferry service, it was inserted into the structure. The bridge would have to be extraordinarily long — 1,350 feet — because the rising waters had so widened the river; rain was, in fact, still falling. A steamer showed up and helped in the ferrying. Despite the intense activity, Sherman recalled, "I have never beheld any work done so quietly, so well." Soon 2,000 men were across.

It was not until the Federal troops began digging entrenchments that the silence was broken. The Quaker who owned the land came rushing up and began berating the soldiers for digging up his farm. They jeered, according to Captain Byers, and the altercation drew a sudden burst of artillery fire from the Confederate batteries. Two men were wounded, and the farmer narrowly escaped injury; Captain Byers recalled that a shell hole "twice as broad as his big hat" opened almost at the farmer's feet.

Around noon the bridge was complete, and about that time General Howard arrived, leading the first regiments of his three divisions now assigned to support Sherman.

Sherman wasted no time. Once his troops had crossed the creek, he deployed them in three infantry columns and, about 1 p.m., sent them up the hill just east of the river. Astonishingly, there was virtually no opposition as the attackers ascended. It was not until they reached the summit that Confederate cannon opened up on them. With great difficulty, Sherman's troops dragged their own artillery to the top — the slope was too steep for horses, and the soldiers had to pull the cannon up with ropes. Soon a brisk exchange of shells had begun.

At last, Sherman, peering about in the rain and mist, had his first opportunity to take stock — and now he received a shock. He was on the wrong hill.

Sherman's objective had been the northmost part of Missionary Ridge, known locally as Tunnel Hill because of the railroad tunnel that passed under it. His maps showed Missionary Ridge as a continuous range running almost to the river, and the visual observation of Grant and Sherman a few days before had seemed to confirm this. In fact, the stunned general could now see that there was a sharp break in the ridge, and the hill closest to the river — the one on which he was standing — was a separate eminence. A deep valley separated him from Tunnel Hill. His labors had left him as far from his objective as ever — and he had lost all chance of surprise.

Grimly, Sherman ordered the soldiers to fortify the nameless mound. It was not much use to the Federals, but it would be a threat if the Confederates captured it. As the short November day drew to a close, Sherman's soldiers dug in and prepared for bloody fighting on the morrow.

Artist's Gallery of Triumph and Tragedy

As bitter fighting broke out around Chattanooga in the autumn of 1863, an English-born artist named James Walker made his way to the scene. Camping with the Army of the Cumberland, Walker sketched and painted battles from Chickamauga to Lookout Mountain and Missionary Ridge.

Union officers made every amenity available to their guest, already a well-known combat artist whose pictures hung in the U.S. Capitol. Walker was indeed among friends. At the outbreak of the Mexican War in 1846 he had been a struggling young art teacher living in Mexico City, and he volunteered his services as an interpreter to the U.S. expeditionary force. Many of the Federal officers at Chattanooga had known Walker in Mexico. What is more, Walker's painting of the Battle of Chapultepec during that campaign — the work that had launched his career as an artist — was famous among military men.

In Tennessee, Walker approached the problem of depicting the rugged, heavily wooded battlefields with the meticulous craftsmanship he had perfected in Mexico. Riding alongside commanding officers, he sketched the combat as it unfolded. Later, when the smoke of battle had cleared, he returned to the site to paint detailed oil sketches of the terrain. Finally, Walker combined action and setting in sweeping canvases, several of which appear here and on the following pages.

Encamped on the steep slopes of Lookout Mountain, James Walker (*left*) and his young protégé Theodore Davis prepare sketches of the battlefield. Davis, an artist for *Harper's Illustrated Weekly* magazine, organized a fund-raising drive to finance Walker's famous painting of the fighting on Lookout Mountain.

In his painting of the Battle of Chickamauga, Walker captures the critical action on Snodgrass Hill during the afternoon of September 20, 1863. Gesturing from his horse in the middle distance (*center*), General George Thomas rallies General John Brannan's bloodied division against the unceasing assaults of General Longstreet's Confederates (*background*). Only the timely arrival of General James Steedman's reserves (*far right*) averted a Federal rout.

While three Union divisions advance toward Lookout Mountain on November 24, 1863, General Hooker, riding a white horse at center, directs artillery fire on Confederate emplacements low on the fog-shrouded slopes. His greatest challenge, Hooker later claimed, was to curb his eager troops' "disposition to engage, regardless of circumstances and, it appears, of consequences."

Depicted as fearlessly reconnoitering the field in the heat of battle, General Hooker confers with an infantryman while his staff officers prudently take shelter behind shell-torn pine trees. Walker, according to some critics, exaggerated the valor of Hooker, who commissioned the battle scene below at a cost of $20,000.

Union cavalrymen graze their horses, and a freight train chugs along the base of Lookout Mountain in this idyllic postcombat painting of the battlefield. The work actually served as a preliminary sketch for the Lookout Mountain battlescape (*pages 126-127*). Walker transformed the locomotive's smoke into the smoke of Confederate muskets.

With the confident air of victors, Union staff officers chat idly as they descend Lookout Mountain after the battle. The Union triumphs here and on nearby Missionary Ridge, just beyond the Tennessee River in the background, broke the Confederate grip on Chattanooga.

Decision on Missionary Ridge

"The scene of disorder beggars description. It was difficult for those acquainted with the unflinching bravery of these same soldiers to realize, much less to understand, the unaccountable, shameful panic which seized them, and for which no apology could be found."

CAPTAIN IRVING A. BUCK, CLEBURNE'S DIVISION, C.S.A.

It had been a wry comment around the Federal campfires for weeks: "On some fine morning General Hooker is going to take Lookout." Yet despite the inactivity, and despite Joseph Hooker's tarnished reputation, the general was still considered a fighter. Thus, in the gray, wet gloom of dawn on November 24, Hooker's men found themselves in line with 60 rounds of ammunition, one day's rations — and orders to attack Lookout Mountain. "The men had not breakfasted," wrote a soldier of the 149th New York. "This announcement took away their appetites."

Hooker's ultimate objective was not Lookout Mountain itself. He planned instead to advance across Lookout Creek and around the mountain through the narrow gap between its lower slopes and the Tennessee River. If he saw an opportunity, he would take the height, but his primary mission was to push beyond it and clear the Confederate forces from the valley between Lookout Mountain and Missionary Ridge. Then he would take possession of Rossville Gap and be in position to threaten the Confederate left and rear.

General Hooker had under his command 10,000 men in three divisions, one from each of the Federal armies on the field: Brigadier General John Geary's division of Hooker's own XII Corps, Brigadier General Charles Cruft's division of IV Corps in the Army of the Cumberland and a division of Sherman's

XV Corps commanded by Brigadier General Peter J. Osterhaus.

Hooker began the movement across Lookout Creek around 8 a.m. He had determined to surprise the Confederates by attacking from two directions. He therefore divided his forces, sending Geary — with his division plus one of Cruft's two brigades, commanded by Brigadier General Walter C. Whitaker — south to Wauhatchie, where the creek was fordable.

There, near the scene of Geary's night battle with Longstreet's brigades, the Federals waded across, taking prisoner 40 Confederate pickets and driving off the rest. With his men feeling their way blindly through the dense fog that shrouded the mountain, Geary led his troops halfway up the western slope. Then they began to work their way northward, along the base of an almost vertical cliff, toward a rendezvous with the rest of the Federal force at the gap between mountain and the river. Enemy resistance had been light so far, but the march was "laborious and extremely toilsome," General Whitaker reported later, "over the steep, rocky, ravine-seamed, torrent-torn sides of the mountain."

Meanwhile Osterhaus' division and Cruft's other brigade, under Colonel William Grose, crossed a bridge a mile and a half north of the ford that Geary had used. The opposing pickets stationed around the bridge had been there for days, and they

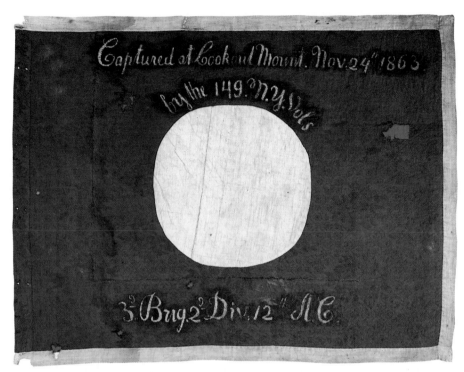

The flag shows the embroidered text: "Captured at Lookout Mount. Nov. 24ʰ 1863 by the 149ᵗ N.Y. Vols" and "3 Brig 2 Div 12ᵗ A.C."

This Confederate flag, carried by a Mississippi regiment in the Battle of Lookout Mountain, was captured during the fighting by Private Peter Kappesser of the 149th New York. The action won fame for Kappesser: He was awarded the Medal of Honor.

were by now old friends. One of the advancing Federals called out, "Oh, Johnny Reb! Johnny Reb!" When a Confederate soldier started forward in amicable response, the Federal cried out, "Go back, Johnny, go back! We are ordered to fire on you." As the astonished Confederate dived for cover, the attacking infantry opened fire. In addition, Federal batteries west of the creek, and those across the Tennessee on Moccasin Bend, began a supporting cannonade.

At first the Confederates on the slopes of Lookout Mountain were merely amused by the Federal activity. The artillery fire was not very effective because of the fog. The defenders watched, fascinated, as shells hurtled out of the mist below and fell short. "We would holler to them to 'put in more powder' and other ludicrous remarks," recalled Private Robert D. Jamison of the 45th Tennessee. "We were enjoying the fun of our fan-cied security, when suddenly we heard the rattle of small arms."

As Jamison and his comrades soon realized, their feeling of security was entirely illusory. In all, 7,000 Confederates were on Lookout Mountain—a force of sufficient strength to fend off many times their number had they been concentrated at the point of the Federals' attack. But the troops were scattered all over the mountain. Only a fraction was in position to defend the plateau at the north end of the height.

Moreover, the general in charge of the Confederate forces on Lookout was unfamiliar with the terrain and the deployment of his troops. Earlier, Braxton Bragg had moved General William Hardee and most of his corps from Lookout Mountain to Missionary Ridge to deal with Sherman's threat. As a result General John Breckinridge, commanding Bragg's other corps, had to extend his left to cover Lookout. That assignment went to the capable Major General Carter L. Stevenson, but he did not arrive on the mountain until after dark on the 23rd. Details of the defense had been left to a lackluster division commander, Brigadier General John K. Jackson.

Worse for the defenders, Hooker's plan of attack was working with remarkable precision, despite the fog and the difficult terrain. About 10 a.m. Geary's troops rounded the shoulder of the mountain at the Cravens farm and made contact with the Confederate defenders under Brigadier General Edward C. Walthall. As sharp fighting erupted, Geary anchored his right on the base of the cliffs rising above the farm and wheeled his line forward until his left smoothly joined with the right flank of Osterhaus' arriving division. Now the Federal line extended

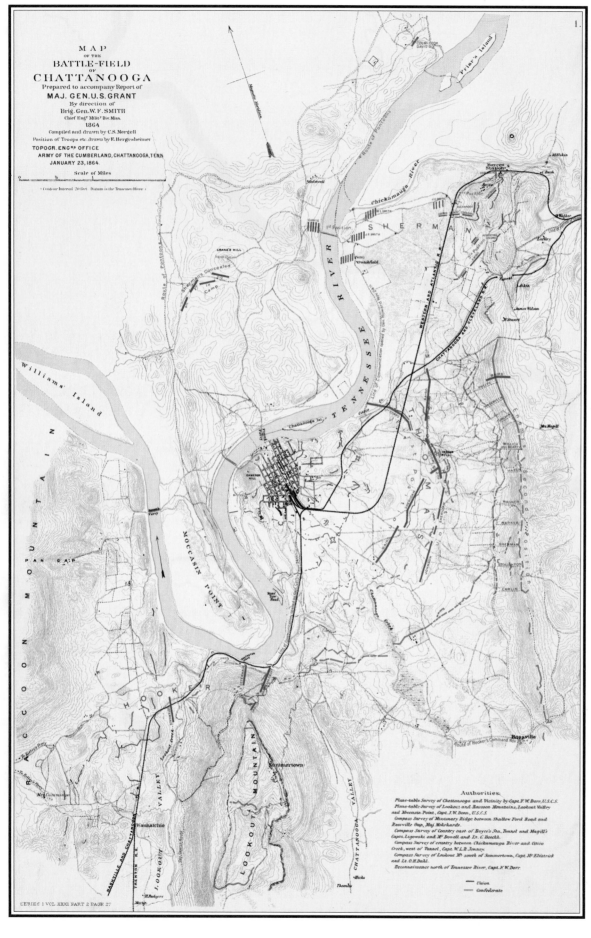

MAP
OF THE
BATTLE-FIELD
OF
CHATTANOOGA
Prepared to accompany Report of
MAJ. GEN. U.S. GRANT
By direction of
Brig. Gen. W. F. SMITH
Chief Eng.ʳ Milit.ʸ Div. Miss.
1864
Compiled and drawn by C.S. Mergell
Position of Troops etc. drawn by F. Hergesheimer
TOPOGR. ENG.ᴿˢ OFFICE
ARMY OF THE CUMBERLAND, CHATTANOOGA, TENN.
JANUARY 23, 1864

Scale of Miles

Contour Interval 20 feet. Datum is the Tennessee River.

This official U.S. Army map, drawn for General Grant, shows the Confederate entrenchments and the dispositions of Federal troops during the final battles of the Chattanooga Campaign. After Hooker's divisions captured Lookout Mountain and gained control of the Chattanooga Valley beyond, the forces of Thomas and Sherman began their drive to push the Confederates from Missionary Ridge.

Authorities:
Plane-table Survey of Chattanooga and Vicinity by Capt. F. W. Dorr, U.S.C.S.
Plane-table Survey of Lookout and Raccoon Mountains, Lookout Valley
and Moccasin Point, Capt. J. W. Donn, U.S.C.S.
Compass Survey of Missionary Ridge between Shallow Ford Road and
Rossville Gap, Maj. Mohrhardt.
Compass Survey of Country east of Boyce's Sta. Tunnel and Magill's,
Capts. Lzgowski and Mc Dowell and Lt. C. Boechk.
Compass Survey of country between Chickamauga River and Citico
Creek, west of Tunnel, Capt. W. L. B. Jenney.
Compass Survey of Lookout Mt. south of Summertown, Capt. Mc Elintrick
and Lt. C. H. Dahl.
Reconnaissance north of Tennessee River, Capt. F. W. Dorr.

Union
Confederate

SERIES I VOL XXXI PART 2 PAGE 27

about a half mile from the Cravens farm down the slope to the Chattanooga road at the foot of the mountain.

To resist the advance of this 10,000-man line, Walthall had only 1,489 troops in breastworks athwart the narrow passage between the mountain and the Tennessee River. And the Confederate gunners on the summit now found to their dismay that they could not depress their cannon enough to be of any help to Walthall. The Federal batteries, moreover, had found the range and were delivering a punishing barrage. The Confederates had been taken completely by surprise, and scores of them were captured before they could fire a shot. Walthall, realizing his predicament, called for reinforcements from General John C. Moore farther to the right.

But support was late in coming. Moore's men had a difficult time finding their way in the fog. In the meantime, the Federals attacked again and again: "Our fire was delivered in continuous volleys," Geary reported, "and, with walls of steel, colors and men were over the works and hand to hand disputed the enemy's possession of them." Walthall's men yielded grudgingly. By 1 p.m., after three hours of fighting, the Confederates had been driven roughly 400 yards east of the Cravens house, into a second line of entrenchments. Around that time Moore's men, groping their way forward in the fog, arrived off to Walthall's right, found the trenches there occupied by Federals and had to fight their way into them. Moore was impressed by his enemy: "I have never before seen them fight with such daring and desperation."

At 1:30 p.m. a fresh Confederate brigade under Brigadier General Edmund W. Pettus appeared on the scene, having been ordered down from the mountaintop by General Jackson. By that time Walthall was in the most desperate straits. According to Pettus, Walthall reported "that he had lost a large part of his command; that his ammunition was nearly exhausted, and that he could not hold the position."

Under fierce, unrelenting fire, Pettus' brigade relieved Walthall's and moved into line beside Moore's troops. Walthall fell back, re-formed and resupplied his men, then waded back into the fight on the left of Pettus' position, where the Federal pressure had been heaviest all day.

Earlier, Walthall had countered that pressure by placing four companies of sharpshooters on the high ground at the base of the cliffs; Federals had driven the riflemen away and now occupied the prime position, firing with lethal effect down on the defenders. At Walthall's suggestion, Pettus sent the 20th Alabama scrambling upward to the left. In fierce fighting they managed to reoccupy the slope and again direct fire on the attackers below; and with the help of the Alabamians, the battered Confederate line was able to stand fast.

The Federals were growing weary and short of ammunition. Night was coming fast, the gloom hastened by the persistent fog—which at least once during the day had stopped the engagement entirely because the soldiers simply could not see where their enemy was. A brigade dispatched by General George Thomas struggled up the mountain, each man laden with as many cartridges as he could carry. But by the time Thomas' reinforcements arrived, it had become too dark to continue fighting.

The battle for Lookout Mountain had

In this dramatic lithograph, dawn pierces clouds and mist obscuring Lookout Mountain as jubilant Union soldiers ascend the slopes on their way to a victory. Grant belittled the victory, considering it a minor action, but the capture of the height was, for many, the symbolic end of the long siege of Chattanooga.

been followed with intense interest by the Federal forces on the plain below. "Hooker's operations were not visible to us except at moments when the clouds would rise," recalled General Grant, who had moved his field headquarters to Orchard Knob. "But the sound of his artillery and musketry was heard incessantly."

In the weeks since Chickamauga, Lookout Mountain—looming, one correspondent said, like "an everlasting thunderstorm"—had taken on a sinister character. In Confederate hands, the great mountain was a malevolent force that had kept Thomas' Army of the Cumberland bottled up and starving in Chattanooga. During all those weeks, there had not been a man in that army who had not prayed for the day when the enemy would be driven off the peak for good.

At dusk, the clouds blew away. "A grand sight was old Lookout that night," said Lieutenant Colonel Joseph S. Fullerton, General Gordon Granger's chief of staff. There were "the parallel fires of the two armies, extending from the summit of the mountain to its base, looking like streams of burning lava, while in between, the flashes from the skirmishers' muskets glowed like giant fireflies."

That night, staring at the cold, clear sky, the soldiers of the two armies were treated to a rare sight: an almost total eclipse of the moon. It was viewed on both sides as a bad omen—for the Confederates. Major James Connolly, serving in Thomas' army as General Absalom Baird's aide, wrote that he and his comrades decided that the eclipse was a bad sign for Bragg "because he was perched on the mountaintop, nearest the moon." And Private Ralph J. Neal of the Confederate 20th Tennessee reported that the eclipse

left him and his friends stricken with a sense of "impending disaster."

As the sky lightened over the peak on November 25, the delighted Federal troops on the slopes below discovered that the Confederates had departed during the night; Bragg had glumly concluded that his troops had little chance of holding the contested gap, and he feared that they would be flanked— perhaps cut off and annihilated—the next morning. Too, he anticipated a heavy attack from Sherman on the right flank, and so in the darkness he shifted his troops to Hardee's command on the north end of Missionary Ridge.

At first light, Captain John Wilson and five men from the 8th Kentucky climbed unopposed to the summit of Lookout Mountain and staged a thrilling pageant. Just before sunrise, carrying a furled U.S. flag, they stepped out onto an overhanging rock. They waited for the sun, and just as its rays hit the peak, the men let loose the flag— to the great delight of the thousands watching from below.

There were wild cheers from Chattanooga Valley, the town itself and the Federal-held hills. "The pealing of the bands," said an English observer, Henry Yates Thompson, "was as if all the harps of Heaven were filling the dome with triumphant music." And James Connolly said feelingly, "Lookout was ours, never again to be used as a perch by rebel vultures."

The frowning eminence of Lookout Mountain had been well publicized throughout the North during the Chattanooga siege, and news of its conquest generated intense excitement in the Union. The event soon became enshrined in legend as the Battle above the Clouds; and by his capture of the famous mountain, Joseph Hooker took a step toward regaining the reputation that had been tarnished at Chancellorsville.

But Lookout had not been a major battle—it was more like a "magnificent skirmish," said the news reporter Sylvanus Cadwallader—and Federal losses had been remarkably light, about 480 men in all. (A brigade commander, noting that his unit's casualties totaled only 56, felt compelled to apologize for the figure. "It is small," he admitted in his report. "The day was dark, and the men well sheltered with rocks.") Confederate losses were considerably higher—totaling 1,251 men, including 1,054 captured or missing.

Grant later scoffed at the mythology that enveloped the battle. He said reports of a magnificent victory at Lookout Mountain were "one of the romances of the war," and then added: "It is all poetry."

Still, the achievement was not without its rewards. Chief among these was the welcome end to the difficulties of supply. With Lookout back in Federal hands, the complicated Cracker Line was no longer necessary. Trains could run unimpeded from Bridgeport to Chattanooga, and steamers could once again follow the river all the way into the city (they were cordelled—pulled by towlines—through The Suck).

General Hooker's troops were now available for further fighting, and Grant immediately ordered them to set out for Rossville Gap in Missionary Ridge to find—and attack—Bragg's left flank.

At first light on the same day, Sherman had pushed his skirmishers toward his objective, Tunnel Hill. Sherman enjoyed an overwhelming superiority of numbers. He had

General Joseph Hooker (*third from right*) confers with members of his staff on a lower slope of Lookout Mountain around the time of the battle. Hooker's victory there brought him to the apex of his career. Within a year, after being passed over as commander of the Army of the Tennessee, Hooker bitterly asked to be relieved of duty in what he called "an army in which rank and service are ignored."

six divisions totaling 26,000 men against only 10,000 troops in the two Confederate divisions under Patrick Cleburne and Carter Stevenson, who had arrived during the night from Lookout Mountain. But the rugged terrain, which greatly favored the defenders, helped to compensate for the Confederate deficit in numbers.

In order to reach the Confederate line a half mile away, Sherman's troops would have to descend the hill that they had occupied, plunge into a little valley, cross an open field under fire, then climb a steep slope against troops who were dug in behind log-and-earth breastworks.

Sherman encountered annoying problems merely in the deploying of his troops in the difficult terrain, and it was not until midmorning that he was able to take the offensive. But even then his attacks were piecemeal and poorly coordinated.

About 10 a.m., after having smoked several cigars while he was prowling his lines, Sherman signaled the advance with a laconic word to his brother-in-law and 4th Division commander, Brigadier General Hugh Ewing: "I guess, Ewing, if you're ready you might as well go ahead."

Ewing launched one of his brigades, under Brigadier General John A. Corse, straight at the forbidding side of Tunnel Hill while Colonel John M. Loomis' brigade moved southward along the western base of the ridge toward the tunnel. Another division would follow Ewing's in reserve, while a third would angle off toward the north and try to turn the Confederate right.

The Federals would face a strong, compact line fashioned by Patrick Cleburne. Secured on the left by Stevenson's division, which had filed into place south of the tunnel, Cleburne's line ran north for several hundred yards, following the ridge of Tunnel Hill to its summit; then the defenses angled sharply eastward to run along a spur that descended to Chickamauga Creek. Cleburne bolstered the line with artillery batteries at three key positions: on the ridge directly above the tunnel, in the angle at the summit and in the north-facing leg of the line. And to man the breastworks in the crucial center position atop the hill, Cleburne chose the tough Texas brigade of Brigadier General James A. Smith.

As the Federal advance began, Corse's four regiments headed straight for Smith's

Federal troops pick over the battlefield halfway up Lookout Mountain, where the most severe fighting occurred. The ravaged farmhouse of Robert Cravens, which was blasted by Federal artillery fire from Moccasin Bend and stripped clean by wood-scavenging soldiers, stands at right.

Texans; in quick response, all three Confederate batteries opened fire on the blue line. But the Confederate infantry waited. Cleburne had decided not to contest the Federal advance with rifle fire until the enemy was upon his main line. So the soldiers watched the formations approach until, one of the Confederates wrote, "we could see the glittering steel and the flash of the officers' swords in the sunlight." Then the Federals reached the base of the ridge and disappeared from view while they swarmed up the rocky 600-foot incline.

Eighty yards from the Confederate breastworks, Corse's Federals crested a lower ridge and found a series of entrenchments that had been abandoned earlier by the Confederates. There the attackers gathered themselves and launched a charge straight at the angle and the four 12-pounder Napoleons of Lieutenant H. Shannon's Mississippi Battery. Cleburne now gave the signal, and his troops leveled a volley at the approaching Federals. It slowed but did not stop them. And as the Federals drew closer, it became apparent that the angle in the center of Smith's line was a woefully weak spot. The Federal infantry was now able to bring the defenders in the salient under a devastating cross fire. The Confederate gunners bore the brunt of this fire, but they valiantly stood fast. Before long Shannon was wounded, and the highest-ranking survivor was a corporal. But assisted by infantrymen, the crews continued to work their guns furiously, scything great gaps in the Federal formations.

Still the Federals came on, into the teeth of what a soldier in the 6th Iowa called "a terrific storm of musket balls and canister," until Corse's men had pushed to within 50 steps of Cleburne's line. Then two of Smith's Texas regiments stood up, leaped over their protective breastworks and took on the Federals with clubbed muskets and bayonets, driving the attackers back to the trenches on the lower ridge.

General Corse had been badly wounded, as had his opposite number, James Smith. Colonel Charles C. Walcutt took Corse's place and led another charge against the Texans — now commanded by Colonel Hiram B. Granbury. With this attack a few Federals reached the Confederate works, but they died there, and the rest were thrown back yet again. For two hours the struggle continued, the Federals grimly coming on time after time, the Confederates stopping them and then countercharging, with Cleburne himself in the vanguard.

Farther south on Corse's right, Loomis' Federal brigade had encountered two Georgia regiments from Stevenson's division. The outnumbered Georgians, one regiment on each side of the railroad track where it emerged from the tunnel, yielded ground grudgingly as Confederate artillery pounded the advancing Federals. Captain Irving A. Buck, Cleburne's adjutant general, recalled, "Every discharge plowed huge gaps through the lines, which were promptly closed up as these brave troops moved forward with a steadiness and order which drew exclamations of admiration from those who witnessed it." But soon Loomis' troops slowed under the devastating barrage; then they halted and took cover. Since Walcutt's troops had far outdistanced those of Loomis, a gap now existed in the Federal line on the west slope of the hill. In order to close this hole and spur on his stalled offensive, Loomis called for reinforcements.

Two Pennsylvania regiments from XI

Corps clambered up the slope and pitched into the battle, followed by a brigade led by Brigadier General Charles L. Matthies. "I had heard the roar of heavy battle before," wrote Captain Samuel Byers, a Federal veteran of the Vicksburg siege, "but never such a shrieking of cannon balls and bursting of shells as met us on that run. We could see the rebels working their guns, while in plain view other batteries galloped up, unlimbered and let loose upon us. Behind us our own batteries were firing at the enemy over our heads, till the storm and roar became horrible." Matthies' four regiments became mixed and their line ragged, but they inched their way upward until they were tantalizingly close to the Confederate breastworks. Their ranks halted near a burning farmhouse, and there they hung in fearful balance, unable to go one step farther and utterly unwilling to take one step back.

The battle now raged all along the line. Walcutt's men were pouring a withering fire into the center of Cleburne's line — "a continuous sheet of hissing, flying lead," recalled Cleburne, concentrated on "a space of not more than 40 yards."

From a vantage point behind the Federal lines, Wisconsin artilleryman Jenkin Jones observed the carnage: General Matthies with a head wound riding to the rear drenched in blood; Colonel Holden Putnam of the 93rd Illinois shot down while carrying forward the regimental colors; two entire regiments "literally cut to pieces, and their officers all killed or wounded.

"I staid under that hill, listening to the noise and rattle of the fight, mingled with suppressed cheers of charging parties, and the groans of the wounded as they passed in long trains of ambulances, or the lighter wounded hobbling back a-foot with bleeding and mangled limbs."

At 2 p.m. Major General Carl Schurz found Sherman seated on a stone fence overlooking the battlefield, watching the action. "The General was in an unhappy frame of mind," Schurz said, "his hopes of promptly overwhelming the enemy's right flank and thus striking the decisive blow of the battle having been dashed. It was a stinging disappointment. He gave vent to his feelings in language of astonishing vivacity."

The battle continued with an intensity that could not long be borne. About 3 p.m., Cleburne recalled, one of his colonels observed that the men were wasting ammunition and were "becoming disheartened at the persistence of the enemy." At the same time, one of Stevenson's commanders, Brigadier General Alfred Cumming, reported that his men "seemed to be moved by a desire to engage the enemy in hand-to-hand conflict," and he offered to lead a bayonet charge. General Hardee approved.

Cumming sent the 36th and 56th Georgia regiments through a narrow opening in the Confederate breastworks and reassembled the troops under withering fire. Then he led a charge that slammed into General Matthies' left flank.

At that moment, Patrick Cleburne leaped atop the Confederate breastworks and, with a flourish of his sword, led Smith's Texans in a charge on Matthies' center. After 10 minutes of savage hand-to-hand fighting, Matthies' troops were fleeing down the mountainside. His left flank exposed, Loomis was also forced to retreat. The Confederates captured eight flags and 500 prisoners, and the slope was littered with hundreds of Federal dead and wounded. Only Corse's four regi-

Patrick Cleburne, who emigrated from Ireland at the age of 21, was one of only two foreign-born officers to attain the rank of major general in the Confederate Army. His staunch defense of Missionary Ridge enhanced his reputation as the "Stonewall Jackson of the West."

Patrick Cleburne's infantrymen and gunners fire point-blank into the on-rushing lines of William Sherman's Federals at the north end of Missionary Ridge. Against overwhelming odds, Cleburne was able to hold off the Union force even after the rest of the Confederate defenses on the ridge had crumbled.

ments, still under Walcutt, remained on the ridge, slugging it out with the Texans and holding their ground.

At last Sherman called a halt. His army had been stopped cold. After suffering nearly 2,000 casualties his troops were still no closer to taking Tunnel Hill than when they had started. He sent word to Grant that his men could do no more. But to Sherman's message Grant dispatched a two-word response: "Attack again."

Sherman followed orders, but he sent in only 200 men from Brigadier General Joseph Lightburn's brigade. Lightburn's troops fared no better than the other Federals; as they scaled the slope of Tunnel Hill their ranks were cut to pieces by the Confederates' fire, and soon the survivors were reeling back to the Federal lines.

A correspondent standing near Sherman watched him light a fresh cigar, draw deeply on it twice and then turn to an aide.

"Tell Lightburn," the correspondent heard Sherman say, "to entrench and go into position." There would be no more attacks on Tunnel Hill that day.

Grant was convinced that there was no point in sending Thomas against the center of Bragg's line until a Confederate flank had been turned. By midmorning Sherman's failure to make an impression on the Confederate right lent new urgency to Hooker's advance on Bragg's left.

Hooker responded with alacrity to Grant's 10 a.m. order to move on Rossville Gap, and he had his command at Chattanooga Creek before noon. But the Confederates had partially destroyed the bridge over the flooded stream, and it took Hooker three hours to make repairs on the span and get his infantry and artillery across.

Hooker finally arrived at Rossville Gap and attacked the Confederate left around 3 p.m. By that time Breckinridge, confident of the strength of the Confederate center but worried about his left, had determined to take personal command of the far left flank, defended by Brigadier General Henry D. Clayton's Alabama brigade. Meanwhile Bragg took direct control of Breckinridge's other two divisions.

Breckinridge arrived to find a rapidly developing disaster. Hooker's forces had driven two of Clayton's regiments from Rossville Gap, and Cruft's Federal division had gained a foothold on the southern slope of Missionary Ridge itself. Just as Breckinridge took command of Clayton's remaining two regiments, Cruft attacked again. Breckinridge was heavily outnumbered, and his line to the immediate north had been thinned to reinforce Cleburne; unable to get additional troops, he could do nothing more than fall back as slowly as possible.

While Geary's division struck the Confederates from the west and Peter Osterhaus' troops went around to the enemy rear through the gap, Cruft's men drove north, onto the crest of the ridge. The Federals routed the defenders, taking hundreds of prisoners, among them Breckinridge's son, Cabell, who was serving as an aide to his father. Finally, the destruction of the Confederate flank that Grant had been looking for was under way; but it was Hooker, not Sherman, who was accomplishing it.

Grant and his aides were still attempting to watch the unfolding events from Orchard Knob. The Confederates defending Missionary Ridge had found the range of the little hill by now, and artillery shells were landing uncomfortably close. "When we saw them coming," recalled Charles Dana, one of the watchers, "we would duck—that is, everybody did except Generals Grant and Thomas and Gordon Granger. It was not according to their dignity to go down on their marrow bones."

The crest of Missionary Ridge was in clear sight. "Bragg's headquarters," said Grant, "were in full view, and officers—presumably staff officers—could be seen coming and going constantly." Grant also thought he could see Confederate reinforcements— "column after column"—being rushed to Cleburne. In this he was mistaken, but the prospect worried him. With darkness not far off, he decided to wait no longer but to send Thomas forward immediately to relieve the pressure on Sherman. Still lacking confidence in the Army of the Cumberland, Grant gave Thomas only a limited objective: His forces were to take the Confederate rifle pits at the foot of Missionary Ridge and then await further instructions.

Grant had no way of knowing that the obstacle confronting Thomas was far less formidable than it appeared. Bragg had left Breckinridge with only three divisions to defend four miles of line, and he had even further weakened the defenses with faulty command decisions.

Unfamiliar with defensive warfare, Bragg had divided his forces along most of his line, sending half of each regiment into the rifle pits located 200 yards in front of the base of the ridge while deploying the rest on the crest. Then Bragg had issued instructions for the men in the rifle pits, if attacked, to fire one volley and withdraw up the hill — an order that was to have disastrous consequences. Even worse for the Confederates, thanks to an incompetent engineer, the still-unfinished breastworks along the top of the ridge had been laid out incorrectly. They were sited at the geographic crest — the highest elevation — instead of being placed at the so-called military crest, which was the elevation that commanded the maximum field of fire down the slope.

On the Federal side, there was a strange delay in executing Grant's order to attack the rifle pits. The general commanding the attacking corps was Gordon Granger, one of the heroes of the Chickamauga defense; but on this day something curious happened to him. He became so fascinated by the artillery fire from Orchard Knob that he was completely distracted. He took over the operation of some of the cannon himself, "sighting the guns with all the enthusiasm of a boy," recalled Sylvanus Cadwallader, "and shouting with the men whenever a shot had done execution." When an hour had passed and Thomas' men had not yet moved, Grant discovered that Granger had never ordered the attack. Suddenly Granger attracted a good deal of notice. Thomas turned on him abruptly and snapped: "Pay more attention to your corps, sir!" General Grant growled a stinging rebuke. "If you will leave that battery to its captain and take command of your corps," he advised Granger, "it will be better for all of us."

When the order to advance was at last transmitted, Grant said, the move forward began "in an incredibly short time." The men of the much maligned Army of the Cumberland, still resentful of Grant's slights, could hardly wait to attack; "we were crazy to charge," said an Indiana man. Brigadier General William B. Hazen reported afterward that in his brigade "all servants, cooks, clerks found guns in some way" and pushed into the ranks.

Once again, the preliminary formation provided a stunning spectacle. As before, Thomas, the consummate drillmaster, formed his ranks with precision, the lines ruler-straight, bands playing, banners fluttering. The troops formed up with Absalom Baird's division on the left, then Thomas Wood's, Philip Sheridan's and Richard Johnson's. When they emerged onto the plain, 20,000 strong, they were a fearsome sight to the Confederates watching from the mountaintop a mile away.

At the signal — six rapid cannon shots from the Federal artillery — the great mass of soldiers started forward, rolling toward the Confederate line with all the ponderous, relentless, menacing force of molten lava. Confederate General Arthur Manigault stared from the crest of Missionary Ridge, "struck," he said, "with the order and regu-

Generals Granger, Grant and Thomas, on a ledge at left, watch from Orchard Knob as their troops swarm up Missionary Ridge in the background. "What was on the summit they knew not," Granger wrote, "and did not inquire. The enemy was before them; to know that was to know sufficient."

larity of their movements" as the Federals approached over the uneven ground.

From both sides of the field came the thunder of artillery. "All our guns, together with those of the enemy all along Missionary Ridge, seemed to open up at once," said a Northern observer. "Such an immense roar I never conceived of. Bragg's headquarters made an irresistible target and was riddled by shot. The Confederate guns, on their part, blasted great holes in the Federal lines." But the attackers continued inexorably forward, while, in the words of another correspondent from a Northern newspaper, "grape and canister and shot and shell sowed the ground with rugged iron and garnished it with the wounded and dead."

The Federals pressed forward without firing, skirmishers in front. Soon the main body broke into a spontaneous run and caught up with the skirmishers. The Confederates held their fire until Thomas' army had marched to within 200 yards. Then they loosed a withering volley that Manigault described as "well-directed and fatal." Yet still the Federals pressed on, and most of the Confederates, obeying Bragg's orders, scurried up the ridge.

This movement proved ruinous for the Confederates: It encouraged the Federals, who thought they were watching their enemy taking flight, and dismayed the defenders higher on the ridge who did not know that the friendly forces were retreating under orders. Furthermore, Bragg's order had not been conveyed to everyone in the rifle pits — some of the Confederates stayed and fought in pointless sacrifice.

The objective was taken, and taken swiftly. Many of the Confederates who had stayed behind were captured. The Federal soldiers lay there, panting but exultant. As the Confederate prisoners were led back toward town, a Union soldier jeered at them, "You've been trying to get there long enough! Now charge on to Chattanooga!"

The Federal gunners ceased firing to avoid hitting their own infantrymen. As the comforting sound of supporting artillery stopped, said a Federal officer, "I never felt so lonesome in my life." Moreover, the triumphant Federals found that they were now exposed to a galling rifle fire from the Confederate entrenchments above them. Colonel John Martin of the 8th Kansas turned to his brigade commander, General August Willich. "We can't live here," he said. A sudden restlessness swept the ranks of men milling at the base of the ridge.

A moment later Grant, watching through his binoculars, saw an astonishing sight. A number of blueclad soldiers were starting up the hill. He watched in disbelief. More men followed. Soon long lines of Federal soldiers could be seen laboriously pushing their way up the slope.

Grant wheeled furiously on Thomas, who was standing beside him. "Thomas," he barked, "who ordered those men up the ridge?" Said the impassive Thomas: "I don't know. I did not." Grant turned fiercely on Granger. "Did you order them up, Granger?" "No," said Granger, "they started without orders." Then, with quiet satisfaction, he added: "When those fellows get started, all hell can't stop them."

His jaw set, Grant returned to his field glasses. He was watching a general's nightmare: a battle gone out of control. He had never contemplated a major assault by Thomas' force. All questions of morale aside, the Army of the Cumberland was

probably no stronger — and possibly weaker — than the Confederate force opposing it on the mountain. Moreover, the center of Bragg's line was presumably its strongest point; certainly the terrain there was forbidding. This unplanned attack against a near-impregnable defensive position was an invitation to disaster.

At one point Grant considered calling the men back. Then he decided to wait a few minutes. "It's all right," an officer heard him mutter, "if it turns out all right." And then he said: "If not, someone will suffer."

As Grant deliberated, the Army of the Cumberland was advancing. Under heavy fire from above, the Federals had — in the felicitous phrase used later by the Comte de Paris, a French nobleman who had served on McClellan's staff — "fled forward," toward their tormentors.

Sheridan, feeling certain that the advance was in violation of orders, had dispatched a staff officer to General Granger asking if it was the first line or the ridge that was to be taken. By the time the messenger returned, confirming that only the first line was to be held, the spontaneous assault was under way. "But, believing that I could carry the ridge," Sheridan recalled, "I could not order those officers and men who were so gallantly ascending the hill to return." Sheridan urged his troops forward. And borrowing a flask from a nearby officer, he waved it at a group of Confederate officers looking down from the hilltop and shouted: "Here's to you!" As he raised the flask to his lips an enemy round burst near him and showered him with dirt. "That is ungenerous," Sheridan growled. "I shall take those guns for that!"

The slope was now a scene of swarming

In these photographs of panels from a lost cyclorama, troops of General Philip Sheridan's division sweep up the slope and across the summit of Missionary Ridge, routing the Confederate defenders. Beyond the wrecked limber in the foreground (*opposite*), the Federals capture an enemy cannon earlier named by the Confederate gun crew "Lady Breckinridge," in honor of the famed General's wife.

activity. In some of the steeper spots, men were scrambling on their hands and knees. Other soldiers, wrote Dana, were "clambering over rocks and through bushes, lifting themselves by thrusting their bayonets into the ground or by catching hold of limbs and twigs." The Federals were heavily burdened, carrying nine-pound muskets as well as 40 rounds of ammunition. In addition, most of the troops were wearing overcoats, for the weather had turned bitter cold. Nevertheless, they scarcely hesitated as they crawled and clawed their way up the incline. A member of Bragg's staff, watching the scene with growing incredulity, concluded that the Federals must be drunk.

The ascending soldiers detected the confusion they were causing among their enemy, and were heartened by it. "Those defending the heights became more and more

desperate as our men approached the top," said an Illinois soldier. "They shouted 'Chickamauga' as though the word itself were a weapon; they thrust cartridges into guns by the handsful, they lighted the fuses of shells and rolled them down, they seized huge stones and threw them, but nothing could stop the force of the charge."

Now the Confederates on the ridge began to suffer again from Bragg's mistakes. The men from the bottom of the slope were racing frantically for the safety of the summit. In the process they were interfering with the defensive fire: The Confederates above were afraid of hitting their own men. Moreover, many of the riflemen in the poorly positioned works now found they could not see the approaching enemy without exposing themselves to Federal fire.

Some of the defenders maintained a savage

147

fusillade. General Manigault, for one, had insisted on laying out his own works and had placed them far enough down the slope to be effective. Captain E. P. Bates of the 125th Ohio recorded, "The most fearful tornado of bursting shells had now passed into a more destructive shower of grape."

But there was something unearthly about those panting climbers. Nothing seemed to daunt them. "Foot by foot and pace by pace," wrote Federal Colonel Charles Harker, whose brigade was in the forefront of the assault, "the crest was being reached to the admiration of all who witnessed it, and to the surprise even of those who participated in the perilous undertaking." The Confederates on Missionary Ridge had demonstrated their courage repeatedly in the months preceding the siege of Chattanooga. But now, as the eerily determined Federals began to reach the crest of the ridge, the resolution of the defenders ebbed. Men threw down their arms and fled, and their panic proved contagious.

Confederate Colonel William F. Tucker watched his brigade crumble: "In spite of the efforts of their officers, they continued to break on each side of the point where the enemy entered our lines until the whole brigade fell back in disorder." The officers of one regiment managed to halt the retreat of their men, "but it was in such a confused mass," recalled a soldier, "that we made but a feeble resistance, when all broke again in a perfect stampede."

Hooker's troops had driven Breckinridge back two and a half miles from his position on the left, almost as far as Bragg's headquarters on the center of the ridge; Breckinridge now joined the commanding general, who was trying to stop the rout. Bragg did what

Crying "On Wisconsin!" Lieutenant Arthur MacArthur Jr. of the 24th Wisconsin snatched up his unit's flag after three color-bearers had been killed and bore the standard to the top of Missionary Ridge. As the story goes, Sheridan himself led the heroic 18-year-old back to his division, saying, "Take care of him. He has just won the Medal of Honor." MacArthur's deeds would later inspire his son, General Douglas MacArthur.

he could. A few moments before, when the Union advance had hesitated at the foot of the hill, he thought that the attack had been stopped. He was riding along the crest waving his hat and congratulating his men when the whole position suddenly caved in around him. He said later: "A panic which I never before witnessed seemed to have seized upon officers and men, and each seemed to be struggling for his personal safety, regardless of his duty and his character."

Repeatedly, Bragg rode up to groups of his fleeing soldiers, standing in their path and crying: "Here's your commander!" But the soldiers only jeered and brushed past.

Breckinridge's response to the chaos around them was more practical, if less soldierly: "Boys," he shouted, "get away the best you can." Indeed, both he and Bragg narrowly escaped capture.

The watchers on Orchard Knob saw the ragged lines of blue reach the crest — in several places at the same time — and, said James Connolly, "in a few moments the flags of 60 Yankee regiments float along Mission Ridge from one end to the other."

A great victory cry swept the ridge as the Federal soldiers realized what they had done. "What yells and cheers broke from the weary but triumphant ranks," recalled Connolly. "They threw their haversacks in the air until it was a cloud of black spots; officers and men mingled indiscriminately in their joy." Some of the soldiers, said Granger's chief of staff, Lieutenant Colonel Fullerton, "madly shouted; some wept from very excess of joy; some grotesquely danced out their delight." General Granger rode gleefully through the celebrating men, shouting: "I'm going to have you all court-martialed! You were ordered to take the works at the foot of the hill and you have taken those at the top! You have disobeyed orders!"

Some Federal officers managed to pull their forces together and continue the drive northward along the crest, flanking the few Confederates who were still holding their ground. Federal soldiers seized batteries and turned the guns on the fleeing Confederates. When no primers could be found, the Federals fired the cannon by shooting muskets over the vents to ignite the charge. Some artillery units attempted to escape, and the Federals shot the horses. Philip Sheridan was seen seated triumphantly astride one of the guns that had almost killed him just a few minutes before. Another officer who tried the same theatrics burned himself on the scorching barrel and was unable to sit down for a fortnight.

The U.S. Army Quartermaster General, Montgomery C. Meigs, had come out from Washington a few weeks before to survey Chattanooga's supply situation in the aftermath of the Confederate siege. At the start of the battle he had been standing with General Grant on Orchard Knob. Now, unaccountably, Major Connolly saw Meigs on Missionary Ridge in the midst of all the jubilation, "wild with excitement, trying himself to wheel one of those guns on the rebels flying down the opposite side of the mountain, and furious because he couldn't find a lanyard with which to fire the gun."

A soldier of the 8th Kansas never forgot the Confederate panic. "Gray-clad men rushed wildly down the hill and into the woods," he said, "tossing away knapsacks, muskets, and blankets as they ran. Batteries galloped back along the narrow, winding roads with reckless speed, and officers, frantic with rage, rushed from one panic-striken group to another, shouting and cursing as they strove to check the headlong flight.

"In ten minutes," continued the Kansan, "all that remained of the defiant rebel army that had so long besieged Chattanooga was captured guns, disarmed prisoners, moaning wounded, ghastly dead, and scattered, demoralized fugitives. Mission Ridge was ours."

But not quite all of it. At the north end of the ridge, General Cleburne was for a time unaware of the disaster that had befallen the rest of the Army of Tennessee. "At our end of the line," said Private John Green of the Orphan Brigade, "we thought the battle had all gone our way." Cleburne's soldiers were actually cheering their victory over Sherman when their corps commander, General Hardee, rode up with word that the Confederate center had collapsed and Cleburne was in danger of being flanked. Cleburne, the only Confederate general involved in the fighting who had not been routed, was charged with protecting the retreat. Slowly and reluctantly, but in good order, he withdrew from

Tunnel Hill and deployed his troops as a rear guard for the broken army.

Sheridan, soon after his arrival at the summit of the ridge, had climbed down from his cannon, rounded up his battered troops — they had suffered 1,304 casualties, more than half the Federal losses in the attack — and led them down the hill after the fleeing Confederates, who were clearly visible on the road leading toward Chickamauga Station. Darkness was descending, but Sheridan captured a number of supply wagons and artillery pieces before he was forced to halt for the night. Grant later credited him with seizing most of the prisoners, artillery and small arms taken on the 25th.

That evening the news of the Federal triumph was telegraphed to Washington. Grant sent a restrained, modestly worded message to General in Chief Halleck: "Although the battle lasted from nearly dawn until dark this evening I believe I am not premature in announcing a complete victory over Bragg. Lookout mountain-top, all the rifle pits in Chattanooga Valley, and Missionary Ridge entire, have been carried, and are now held by us. I have no idea of finding Bragg here tomorrow."

That night, as Cleburne protected their rear, Bragg's demoralized Confederates gathered at Chickamauga Station and made preparations to retreat deep into Georgia. Officers spent the night trying to bring some order to the chaos.

Bragg was distraught. Private Sam Watkins of the 1st Tennessee saw the commanding general at this worst moment of his life and wrote: "I felt sorry for General Bragg. The army was routed and Bragg looked so scared. Poor fellow, he looked so hacked and whipped and mortified and chagrined at de-

feat." Captain Buck, carrying a message to Bragg a little later, found him curiously agitated and unlike himself — obviously suffering, said Buck, from "nervous anxiety."

The Confederates managed to withdraw from Chickamauga Station — aboard trains and on foot — without further damage, but they left behind abundant evidence of their disarray. The first Federal soldiers to arrive at the depot on the following morning found fires everywhere: Shattered wagons, wrecked artillery pieces, discarded pontoons and huge piles of grain were all burning in the streets.

For a time Grant pressed the pursuit. Hooker led the chase, and on the 27th he caught up with Cleburne at Ringgold, Georgia, about 15 miles from Chattanooga. Just beyond Ringgold was a mountain pass so narrow that it barely accommodated, side by side, a railroad track, a stream and a wagon road. Cleburne hid the greater part of his force in this natural trap, while his cavalry lured Hooker into the ambush. As the Federals entered the pass, the Confederates suddenly smashed them with artillery and musket fire.

Hooker's troops reeled. But they quickly recovered, and a fierce engagement followed — small, but hard fought. For six hours, Cleburne held fast. Then, when Bragg's army was at a safe distance, Cleburne adroitly slipped away. He had commanded about 4,200 men in this action, and his losses totaled only 221. Hooker's casualties came to 442 — about the same number that he had lost at Lookout Mountain.

On November 28 Grant finally called an end to the pursuit. The fight for Lookout Mountain and Missionary Ridge — soon to be known collectively as the Battle of Chat-

A Studio on Point Lookout

Not long after the firing died away on Lookout Mountain, an enterprising photographer from Ohio named Royan M. Linn arrived in Chattanooga, seeking to make his fortune from the battle that had already become famous. Linn set up his darkroom on top of the mountain, and for a studio he selected the most breathtaking panorama around— Point Lookout, a majestic pinnacle of rock jutting from the mountainside, beyond which could be seen the shimmering Tennessee River as it snaked its way through the rugged countryside.

Linn did not lack for customers. Federal officers and enlisted men who had fought on the heights around Chattanooga climbed Lookout Mountain in droves to pose daringly on the jutting rock. Over the months, the photographer made thousands of *cartes de visite* for men eager to commemorate their roles in the events that had unfolded on the cruel ridges of the Cumberland.

Royan M. Linn, cane in hand, sits with two of his assistants beside a stereocamera, looking out over the magnificent view he helped to popularize. Even after Linn's death in 1872 his family continued to maintain the studio on the rock.

Portraits on a Pinnacle

OFFICERS OF THE 2ND OHIO
HEAVY ARTILLERY

MEMBERS OF COMPANY F, 7TH ILLINOIS

MAJOR GENERAL JOSEPH HOOKER

THE BAND OF 2ND BRIGADE, 3RD
DIVISION, XXIII CORPS

SOLDIERS FROM MASSACHUSETTS

MEN OF THE 8TH KENTUCKY

tanooga — had not been especially costly in men compared with the War's major battles — Chickamauga, for example. The Confederate casualty total for the three days — 6,700 soldiers killed, wounded or captured — was higher than that of the Union, which lost 5,800 men. Most of the Confederate casualties — 4,100 troops — however, were prisoners taken in the attack on Missionary Ridge; whereas only 350 of the 5,800 Federals were captured.

Grant called off the pursuit of Bragg's forces because the Federal army was low on rations and he did not think it could live off the barren country below Chattanooga. He decided that he must stay close to his supply line. It also had been made clear to Grant that he had a responsibility more urgent than chasing Bragg.

Ambrose Burnside's Army of the Ohio was still besieged by James Longstreet in Knoxville, and Grant had been told that Burnside had only enough rations to last until December 3, now five days away. President Lincoln, Secretary of War Stanton and General Halleck were all clamoring for the rescue of Burnside. "Well done," read Lincoln's message of congratulations to Grant. "Many thanks to all. Remember Burnside." Halleck had dealt with the good news cursorily — "I congratulate you on the success thus far of your plans" — before hastening to the real point of his wire: "I fear that General Burnside is hard-pressed and that any further delay may prove fatal. I know that you will do all in your power to relieve him."

In fact, Grant had taken the first steps toward lifting the siege of Knoxville even before the fighting began at Chattanooga. He had ordered Thomas to send Granger's en-

tire Reserve Corps north as soon as Bragg was no longer a threat.

On November 27, with the Confederate army in full flight, Grant, pursuing his enemy with Hooker, sent word to Thomas to get Granger moving. But when Grant returned to Chattanooga on the night of the 29th, Granger was still there. Worse, Grant said in disgust, the corps commander "was reluctant to go, having decided for himself that it was a very bad move to make." Grant thereupon gave command of the expedition to Sherman; the relief force would consist of the Army of the Tennessee plus Granger's corps. Granger himself was transferred to the Department of the Gulf, where he served for the rest of the War.

Then Grant set down on paper his plans for the rescue of Knoxville, and he took pains to see that a copy "in some way or other" fell into Longstreet's hands. If Longstreet understood that an overwhelming force was about to descend on him, he might depart without further bloodshed.

Sherman's men were exhausted, undernourished, and short of equipment. Sherman nevertheless took them on a grueling 85-mile forced march to reach Knoxville before Burnside ran out of supplies. Sherman's cavalry vanguard just made the December 3 deadline — to discover that after attacking Fort Sanders four days earlier, Longstreet had in fact decamped upon learning of Sherman's approach.

As for Burnside, he and his men seemed in much better shape than had been anticipated. On his arrival Sherman was taken to a local home where he and Burnside and their staff officers were treated to a roast turkey dinner — served, the fuming Sherman noted, "with clean tablecloth, dishes, knives,

Captured Confederate soldiers are held under guard outside Chattanooga's train station as they wait to be sent north to prison camps. According to General Grant, more than 6,000 Confederates were taken prisoner during the actions at Chattanooga, many during Sheridan's dogged pursuit after the capture of Missionary Ridge.

forks, spoons, etc." Burnside cheerfully explained that the Tennesseans had been keeping his forces adequately supplied and that they had never been in any serious danger of starvation. The reports of Burnside's plight had somehow been greatly exaggerated.

Although Sherman was irate — and made no secret of it — his arduous march had served its purpose. Perhaps Knoxville had not been starving, but it had certainly been besieged. Now, having driven Longstreet away, Sherman and his men made a leisurely march back to Chattanooga.

Burnside, strengthened by Granger's corps, briefly pursued Longstreet into the easternmost mountains of Tennessee. Then, much to the annoyance of Grant, Burnside gave up the chase and returned to Knoxville. Longstreet remained in Tennessee, but his Confederates were no longer a threat;

they would slip away after a hard winter.

Meanwhile, on November 28 Braxton Bragg had reported to Richmond on the state of his command and had closed with the words: "I deem it due to the cause and to myself to ask for relief from command and an investigation into the causes of the defeat." Two days later, his resignation as head of the Army of Tennessee was accepted by Jefferson Davis, and William J. Hardee took over as commander.

Confederate forces would return to Tennessee. But the South would never recover from the effects of the fighting around Chattanooga. The gateway to the heart of the Confederacy had been flung open; and by the banks of the Tennessee River, William Tecumseh Sherman was already starting to think about a Federal advance on the city of Atlanta in the spring.

Building a Union Bastion

Almost before the last gray uniform had disappeared south into Georgia in December of 1863, General Grant and his lieutenants began turning Chattanooga into a massive supply depot and staging base for a new Union offensive. It was a formidable task. The Confederate siege had left the town isolated and bereft. The Federal soldiers encamped on its streets and hillsides had subsisted for weeks on quarter rations; trees, fences and even frame houses had been leveled for firewood, and anything green had long since been cropped by the army's famished horses and mules.

The first priority was to restore Chattanooga's severed supply lines to the North. By January of 1864, new bridges were spanning rivers and creeks, roadways had been repaired and the railroads were running again. Soon locomotives and freight cars, commandeered from all over the Union, were delivering a torrent of arms, animals and provisions. Before the spring, Chattanooga had become a bulging arsenal from which Grant's successor, Major General William Tecumseh Sherman, would launch an army of 100,000 men against the next Federal objective: Atlanta.

Beneath the distinctive profile of Lookout Mountain, Chattanooga after the siege presents a motley array of Union army tents and frame buildings. At rear left i

Atop Lookout Mountain, officers of General Joseph Hooker's command relax under the gingerbread eaves of the house that Hooker took for his headquarters after the Federals stormed the mountain. Before the War the Victorian-style lodge had been part of a resort community popular with Southern families for its cool breezes and spectacular view.

the vaulted roof of the railroad depot, built before the War by slave labor, and on a hill to its right are the barracks-like structures of a new military hospital.

Portions of the Chattanooga countryside have been stripped bare for fuel and forage in this 1864 view looking west toward Cameron Hill. "When I first came here the hi

Federal soldiers stand at ease outside the modest house used as headquarters for the Army of the Cumberland. Major General George H. Thomas remained on duty here through Christmas of 1863 while most of his officers and men took holiday leave. "Something is sure to get out of order if I go away," Thomas grumbled. "It was always so."

...as covered with very large cedar trees," wrote a civilian visitor. "They have now disappeared — stumps and all — for firewood."

Settled in for garrison duty at newly established Fort Sherman on the elevated eastern edge of Chattanooga, the men of Battery C, 1st Wisconsin Heavy Artillery, form up at the foot of their company street. At left and rear, the soldiers' laundry hangs out to dry.

A well-bundled Union sentinel in Chattanooga is silhouetted against trees laden with snow. The harsh weather kept the Federal troops from venturing far from the city. "The winter of 1863-64 opened very cold and severe," wrote a frustrated General William T. Sherman, "and it was manifest that military operations must in a measure cease."

A Federal army work gang operates a sawmill on Lookout Mountain after the height was captured by Federal troops. Lookout's virgin forest provided hardwood sorely needed to restore bridges, construct fortifications and fuel campfires.

Empty stables await the arrival of fresh horses for the spring campaign. Starvation and overwork had taken a devastating toll of the army's animals: "They are driven," wrote General John Beatty, "until they drop and are abandoned to die in the mudhole where they fall."

Men of the Federal Quartermaster Corps stand ready to transfer sacks of grain from the steamboat *Kingston* to waiting wagons at Chattanooga. The *Kingston*, armed with a cannon on its bow, had safely completed the voyage from Bridgeport, with food for the army's bone-thin horses and men.

164

Riverboats lie moored to rough wharves along the Tennessee River after bringing supplies to Chattanooga. General Grant was trying to fill the army's warehouses here and at Nashville with a six-month supply of stores and ammunition to sustain a spring drive into Georgia.

A military construction crew works to extend a new wagon bridge over the Tennessee River to Chattanooga (*background*) in early 1864. The engineers built abutments of fresh-hewn logs and used the new fish-shaped trusses, called "shad bellies," to support each section of the span.

The completed bridge, seen from the Chattanooga side of the river, helped open the town to overland supply and reinforcement from the North. A drawbridge section along the near shore enabled small steamboats to pass through.

When this railroad to Nashville reopened in January 1864, enough supplies got through to enable the Federal army in Chattanooga to go on full rations f

A turreted blockhouse guards a railroad bridge over the Hiawassee River between Knoxville and Chattanooga in 1864. The fortification was one of at least 100 small works erected to protect bridges and tunnels in eastern Tennessee from Confederate raids and from what General Sherman called "the acts of a hostile local population."

Officials of the United States Military Railroads Construction Corps, dispatched from Washington, display the rudimentary tools of railroad building and repair. The 300-man detachment helped fulfill General Sherman's requirement that 130 freight cars, carrying 10 tons apiece, reach Chattanooga daily.

the first time since the Battle of Chickamauga.

The Federal engineers' proud achievement, a 780-foot-long trestle bridge rushed to completion early in 1864, spans Running Water Ravine near Wauhatchie

Tennessee, on the Nashville & Chattanooga Railroad. In the foreground, builders perch on the wreckage of an earlier bridge, destroyed by the Confederates.

PICTURE CREDITS

Cover: Painting by Douglas Volk, Minnesota Historical Society, on loan to the Minnesota State Capitol, photographed by Gary Mortensen. 2, 3: Maps by Peter McGinn. 8, 9: Special Collections (Orlando Poe Collection), U.S. Military Academy Library, copied by Henry Groskinsky. 10-15: Library of Congress. 16, 17: National Archives Neg. No. 111-B-4866. 19: William L. Clements Library, University of Michigan. 20: Painting by William Travis, Smithsonian Institution, Washington, D.C., Photo No. 49433-H. 22: Mississippi Department of Archives and History, from *Van Dorn: The Life and Times of a Confederate General*, by Robert G. Hartje, published by Vanderbilt University Press, Nashville, 1967. 23: Michigan Department of State, State Archives. 25: Library of Congress. 26, 27: From *The Photographic History of the Civil War*, Vol. 2., edited by Francis Trevelyan Miller, published by The Review of Reviews Co., New York, 1911. 28: Courtesy Seward R. Osborne. 29: Engraving by J.T.E. Hillen, from *The Soldier in Our Civil War: A Pictorial History of the Conflict, 1861-1865*, edited by Paul F. Mottelay and T. Campbell-Copeland, published by G. W. Carleton & Company, New York, 1886. 30, 31: Painting by Horace Rawdon, courtesy Frank F. Marvin. 35: Confederate Memorial Hall, New Orleans. 36, 37: Paintings by William Travis, Smithsonian Institution, Washington, D.C., Photo Nos. 49432-G; 49431-D. 38: From *The Photographic History of the Civil War*, Vol. 2, edited by Francis Trevelyan Miller, published by The Review of Reviews Co., New York, 1911. 40, 41: Mississippi State Historical Museum, Mississippi Department of Archives and History, Jackson, photographed by Gib Ford, except photograph Mississippi Department of Archives and History, Jackson. 43: The Western Reserve Historical Society, Cleveland, Ohio. 45: Tennessee State Museum, photographed by Bill LaFevor. 46: Sketch by Alfred R. Waud, Library of Congress. 47: Valentine Museum, Richmond, Virginia. 49: Map by Walter W. Roberts. 50, 51: Painting by Alfred Thorsen, State Historical Society of Wisconsin. 53: Sketch by Alfred R. Waud, from *The Mountain Campaigns in Georgia*, by Jos. M. Brown, published by Matthews, Northrup & Co., Buffalo, N.Y., 1890. 56: Library of Congress. 57: Map by Walter W. Roberts. 58, 59: Inset Old State House, Little Rock, Arkansas — sketch by Walton Taber, Tennessee State Museum, photographed by Bill LaFevor. 60: Sketch by Frank Vizetelly, by permission of the Houghton Library. 62: Library of Congress — Massachusetts Commandery, Military Order of the Loyal Legion of the United States and the U.S. Army Military History Institute (MASS/MOLLUS/USAMHI), copied by A. Pierce Bounds — courtesy Erick Davis Collection; courtesy Mark Katz, Americana Image Gallery. 63: National Archives Neg. No. 165-JT-189 — Allen Cebula Collection at the U.S. Army Military History Institute, copied by A. Pierce Bounds — from *The Civil War Letters of Colonel Hans Christian Heg*, edited by Theodore C. Blegen, published by Norwegian-American Historical Association, Northfield, Minnesota, 1936; from *History of the Sixth Regiment Indiana Volunteer Infantry*, by Charles C. Briant, published by Wm. B. Burford, Indianapolis, 1891. 65: Library of Congress. 66, 67: Painting by Harry J. Kellogg, Minnesota Historical Society. 68: Courtesy Bill Turner. 69: Map by Walter W. Roberts. 70, 71: Inset Library of Congress; courtesy Frank & Marie-T. Wood Print Collections, Alexandria, Virginia; inset photograph by Carl C. Giers (1828-1877) courtesy Sarah Hunter Green and C. William Green II. 72, 73: Library of Congress. 74, 75: Rifles (2) War Library and Museum, MOLLUS, photographed by Larry Sherer; courtesy of The Cincinnati Historical Society — courtesy C. Paul Loane, copied by Arthur Soll. 76, 77: War Library and Museum, MOLLUS, photographed by Larry Sherer. 79: James C. Frasca Collections, photographed by Andy Cifranic. 80: Sketch by J.T.E. Hillen, Print Collection, The New York Public Library, Astor, Lenox and Tilden Foundations. 81: MASS/MOLLUS/USAMHI, copied by A. Pierce Bounds. 82, 83: The Western Reserve Historical Society, Cleveland, Ohio. 84: Photograph by J. W. Campbell, Chicago Historical Society, Neg. No. ICHi-10484. 86, 87: Anne S. K. Brown Military Collection, Brown University Library. 90, 91: From *The Photographic History of the Civil War*, Vol. 10, edited by Francis Trevelyan Miller, published by The Review of Reviews Co., New York, 1912; MASS/MOLLUS/USAMHI, copied by A. Pierce Bounds; sketch by Theodore R. Davis, courtesy American Heritage Picture Collection. 92: Painting by William Travis, Smithsonian Institution, Washington, D.C., Photo No. 49432-D. 94: Sketch by Frank H. Schell, Print Collection, The New York Public Library, Astor, Lenox and Tilden Foundations — Minnesota Historical Society. 96, 97: Tennessee State Museum, photographed by Bill LaFevor. 98: Courtesy Joseph H. Bergeron. 101: The Frank H. McClung Museum, The University of Tennessee-Knoxville, photographed by W. Miles Wright. 102, 103: Library of Congress. 105: Courtesy Jerry E. Keyes, copied by W. Miles Wright. 106, 107: National Archives Neg. Nos. 165-C-203; 165-C-202. 108, 109: Courtesy Frank & Marie-T. Wood Print Collections, Alexandria, Virginia. 110, 111: Courtesy Frank & Marie-T. Wood Print Collections, Alexandria, Virginia — National Archives Neg. Nos. 77-HT-72A-3; 77-HT-72A-4. 112: Courtesy Mark Katz, Americana Image Gallery. 113: Library of Congress. 114, 115: From *The Loyal Mountaineers of Tennessee*, by Thomas William Humes, S.T.D., published by Ogden Brothers & Company, Knoxville, Tennessee, 1888. 116, 117: MASS/MOLLUS/USAMHI, copied by A. Pierce Bounds — Library of Congress. 119: Courtesy Barbara and Robert Brezak — courtesy Jerry E. Keyes, on loan to The Frank H. McClung Museum, The University of Tennessee-Knoxville, photographed by W. Miles Wright. 122: Courtesy Chris Nelson. 124, 125: Inset Chicago Historical Society Neg. No. ICHi-07935 — U.S. Army Center of Military History, photographed by Larry Sherer. 126, 127: Inset N. S. Meyer Collection, photographed by Al Freni — U.S. Army Center of Military History, photographed by Larry Sherer. 128, 129: Inset American National Bank and Trust Co., Chattanooga, Tennessee; West Point Museum Collections, U.S. Military Academy, photographed by Henry Groskinsky. 131: Museum of the Confederacy, Richmond, Virginia, photographed by Larry Sherer. 132: Courtesy Frank & Marie-T. Wood Print Collections, Alexandria, Virginia. 134, 135: Courtesy The New-York Historical Society, New York City. 137: MASS/MOLLUS/USAMHI, copied by Robert Walch. 138: The Western Reserve Historical Society, Cleveland, Ohio. 140: Pastel drawing by Sadie Waters, Tennessee State Museum, photographed by Bill LaFevor. 141: Library of Congress. 144, 145: Painting by Thure de Thulstrup, courtesy Seventh Regiment Fund, Inc., photographed by Al Freni. 146, 147: Photographs by Henry Hamilton Bennett. 148: State Historical Society of Wisconsin. 151: National Archives Neg. No. 77-F-147-2-11. 152: L. M. Strayer Collection — courtesy T. Scott Sanders; Special Collections (Orlando Poe Collection), U.S. Military Academy Library, copied by Henry Groskinsky. 153: The Western Reserve Historical Society, Cleveland, Ohio — courtesy T. Scott Sanders (2). 155: The Western Reserve Historical Society, Cleveland, Ohio. 156, 157: Inset National Archives Neg. No. 111-B-4848 — Chattanooga Museum of Regional History, copied by Michael W. Thomas. 158, 159: Inset National Archives Neg. No. 111-B-4871 — Chattanooga Museum of Regional History, copied by Michael W. Thomas. 160, 161: Inset National Archives Neg. No. 111-B-7029; State Historical Society of Wisconsin. 162, 163: National Archives Neg. Nos. 111-B-4799, inset 111-B-4857. 164, 165: Inset Michigan Department of State, State Archives — Library of Congress. 166, 167: National Archives Neg. Nos. 77-F-147-2 6A; 111-B-6355 — 111-B-2042; 111-B-662. 168, 169: Archives of the University of Notre Dame; insets Library of Congress (2). 170, 171: Archives of the University of Notre Dame.

BIBLIOGRAPHY

Books

Alexander, E. P., *Military Memoirs of a Confederate*. Dayton: Morningside Bookshop, 1977 (reprint of 1907 edition).

Badeau, Adam, *Military History of Ulysses S. Grant*. Vol. 1. New York: D. Appleton and Company, 1885.

Basler, Roy P., ed., *The Collected Works of Abraham Lincoln*. New Brunswick, N.J.: Rutgers University Press, 1953.

Beatty, John, *The Citizen-Soldier*. Cincinnati: Wilstach, Baldwin & Co., 1983 (reprint of 1879 edition).

Blackford, Susan Leigh, comp., *Letters from Lee's Army*. Ed. by Charles Minor Blackford III. New York: Charles Scribner's Sons, 1947.

Buck, Irving A., *Cleburne and His Command*. Dayton: Morningside Bookshop, 1982.

Burr, Frank A., and Richard J. Hinton, *The Life of Gen. Philip H. Sheridan*. Providence: J. A. & R. A. Reid, 1888.

Catton, Bruce:
Grant Takes Command. Boston: Little, Brown, 1968.
This Hallowed Ground. New York: Pocket Books, 1956.

Cleaves, Freeman, *Rock of Chickamauga: The Life of General George H. Thomas*. Norman: University of Oklahoma Press, 1948.

Commager, Henry Steele, ed., *The Blue and the Gray*. New York: Bobbs-Merrill Company, Inc., 1973.

Connelly, Thomas Lawrence:
Army of the Heartland: The Army of Tennessee, 1861-1862. Baton Rouge: Louisiana State University Press, 1967.
Autumn of Glory: The Army of Tennessee, 1862-1865. Baton Rouge: Louisiana State University Press, 1971.

Connolly, James A., *Three Years in the Army of the Cumberland. Ed. by Paul M. Angle. Bloomington: Indiana University Press, 1959.

Dana, Charles A., *Recollections of the Civil War.* New York: D. Appleton and Company, 1902.

Dana, Charles A., and J. H. Wilson, *The Life of Ulysses S. Grant.* Springfield, Mass.: Gurdon Bill & Company, 1868.

Davis, William C., ed., *The Guns of '62.* Vol. 2 of *The Image of War, 1861-1865.* New York: Doubleday & Co., 1982.

Doll, William H., *History of the Sixth Regiment Indiana Volunteer Infantry in the Civil War.* Columbus, Ind.: Republican Job Print, 1903.

Downey, Fairfax, *Storming of the Gateway: Chattanooga, 1863.* New York: David McKay Company, Inc., 1960.

Evans, Clement A., ed., *Confederate Military History.* Vols. 8 and 10. New York: Thomas Yoseloff, 1962.

Foote, Shelby, *The Civil War, a Narrative: Fredericksburg to Meridian.* New York: Random House, 1963.

Freeman, Douglas Southall, *Lee's Lieutenants.* New York: Charles Scribner's Sons, 1944.

Grant, U. S., *Personal Memoirs of U. S. Grant.* New York: Charles L. Webster & Company, 1894.

Green, Johnny, *Johnny Green of the Orphan Brigade.* Ed. by A. D. Kirwan. Lexington: University of Kentucky Press, 1956.

Hartje, Robert G., *Van Dorn: The Life and Times of a Confederate General.* Nashville: Vanderbilt University Press, 1967.

Harwell, Richard B., ed., *The Confederate Reader.* New York: David McKay Company, Inc., 1976.

Heg, Hans Christian, *The Civil War Letters of Colonel Hans Christian Heg.* Ed. by Theodore C. Blegen. Northfield, Minn.: Norwegian-American Historical Association, 1936.

Henry, Robert Selph:
"First with the Most": Forrest. New York: Bobbs-Merrill Company, 1944.
The Story of the Confederacy. Gloucester, Mass.: Peter Smith, 1970.

High, Edwin W., *History of the Sixty-eighth Regiment Indiana Volunteer Infantry 1862-1865.* Published by request of the Sixty-eighth Indiana Infantry Association, 1902.

Hood, J. B., *Advance and Retreat.* New Orleans: G. T. Beauregard, 1880.

Horn, Stanley F., *The Army of Tennessee.* Norman: University of Oklahoma Press, 1952.

Horn, Stanley F., comp. and ed., *Tennessee's War 1861-1865.* Nashville: Tennessee Civil War Centennial Commission, 1965.

Howe, Henry, *Historical Collections of Ohio.* Vols. 2 and 3. Columbus: Henry Howe & Son, 1891.

Johnson, Robert Underwood, and Clarence Clough Buel, eds., *Battles and Leaders of the Civil War.* Vol. 3. New York: Century Co., 1887.

Lamers, William M., *The Edge of Glory: A Biography of General William S. Rosecrans, U.S.A.* New York: Harcourt, Brace & World, Inc., 1961.

Leech, Margaret, and Harry J. Brown, *The Garfield Orbit.* New York: Harper & Row, 1978.

Lewis, Lloyd, *Sherman: Fighting Prophet.* New York: Harcourt, Brace and Company, 1932.

Lytle, Andrew Nelson, *Bedford Forrest and His Critter Company.* New York: G. P. Putnam's Sons, 1931.

McDonough, James Lee, *Chattanooga.* Knoxville: University of Tennessee Press, 1984.

McWhiney, Grady, *Braxton Bragg and Confederate Defeat.* New York: Columbia University Press, 1969.

Madaus, Howard Michael, *The Battle Flags of the Confederate Army of Tennessee.* Milwaukee: Milwaukee Public Museum, 1976.

Manigault, Arthur Middleton, *A Carolinian Goes to War.* Ed. by R. Lockwood Tower. Columbia: University of South Carolina Press, 1983.

Mauzy, James H., comp., *Historical Sketch of the Sixty-eighth Regiment Indiana Volunteers.* Rushville, Ind.: The Republican Co., 1887.

Miller, Francis Trevelyn, ed., *The Photographic History of the Civil War in Ten Volumes.* Vol. 2. New York: The Review of Reviews Co., 1912.

Oates, William C., *The War between the Union and the Confederacy and Its Lost Opportunities.* Dayton: Morningside Bookshop, 1974 (reprint of 1905 edition).

O'Connor, Richard, *Sheridan: the Inevitable.* New York: Bobbs-Merrill Company, Inc., 1953.

Rowell, John W., *Yankee Artillerymen.* Knoxville: University of Tennessee Press, 1975.

Seymour, Digby Gordon, *Divided Loyalties: Fort Sanders and the Civil War in East Tennessee.* Knoxville: University of Tennessee Press, 1963.

Strode, Hudson, *Jefferson Davis: Confederate President.* New York: Harcourt, Brace and Company, 1959.

Todd, William, *The Seventy-ninth Highlanders New York Volunteers in the War of Rebellion 1861-1865.* Albany: Brandow, Barton & Co., 1886.

Truxall, Aida Craig, ed., *"Respects To All": Letters of Two Pennsylvania Boys in the War of the Rebellion.* Pittsburgh: University of Pittsburgh Press, 1962.

Tucker, Glenn, *Chickamauga.* Dayton: Morningside Bookshop, 1976.

United States War Department, *War of the Rebellion: A Compilation of the Official Records of the Union and Confederate Armies.* Series 1 — Vols. 23, 30, 31 and 38. Government Printing Office, 1889-1891.

Upson, Theodore F., *With Sherman to the Sea.* Ed. by Oscar Osburn Winther. Baton Rouge: Louisiana State University Press, 1943.

Warner, Ezra J.:
Generals in Blue: Lives of the Union Commanders. Baton Rouge: Louisiana State University Press, 1964.
Generals in Gray: Lives of the Confederate Commanders. Baton Rouge: Louisiana State University Press, 1959.

Watkins, Samuel R., *"Co. Aytch".* New York: Collier Books, 1962.

Wiley, Bell Irvin, *The Life of Johnny Reb.* New York: Bobbs-Merrill Company, 1943.

Williams, Kenneth P., *Lincoln Finds A General.* Vol. 5. New York: Macmillan Company, 1959.

Williams, T. Harry, *Lincoln and His Generals.* New York: Vintage Books, 1952.

Wyeth, John Allan, *Life of General Nathan Bedford Forrest.* Dayton: Morningside Bookshop, 1975.

Other Sources

"The Army of the Cumberland." *Harper's Weekly,* October 31, 1863.

"Chattanooga." *Harper's Weekly,* November 28, 1863.

Crow, Vernon, "Confederate Indecision and Delay: The Empty Victory at Chickamauga." *The Kepi,* February-March 1984.

Dove, J. N., "Chickamauga — Another Account of General Steedman's Gallantry on That Bloody Field." *National Tribune,* March 13, 1884.

"John L. Clem, Hero of Civil War at 10." *The New York Times,* (obituary) May 15, 1937.

Johnson, Leland R., "Civil War Railroad Defenses in Tennessee." *The Tennessee Valley Historical Review,* Summer 1972.

Johnson, Walter C., *Chattanooga News,* September 20, 1938.

Neel, James F., "William Lytle & the 'Bloody Tinth' Ohio." *Military Images Magazine,* July-August 1981.

"Our Youngest Soldier." *Harper's Weekly,* February 6, 1864.

Smith, William Wrenshall, "Holocaust Holiday." *Civil War Times Illustrated,* October 1979.

Tucker, Glenn, "The Battle of Chickamauga." *Civil War Times Illustrated,* May 1960.

Van Camp, M. H., "Chickamauga — The Stubborn Fight Made by the 21st Ohio." *National Tribune,* September 4, 1884.

Young, J. K., "Chickamauga — The Battle as I Saw It." *National Tribune,* April 22, 1886.

ACKNOWLEDGMENTS

The editors wish to thank the following individuals and institutions for their valuable assistance in the preparation of this volume:

Georgia: Fort Oglethorpe — Edward E. Tinney, Chickamauga-Chattanooga National Military Park.

Michigan: Lansing — John Curry, Michigan State Archives.

Mississippi: Jackson — Lisa Buechele, Mary Lohrenz, Mississippi State Historical Museum.

Ohio: Cleveland — Mary Brooks, Western Reserve Historical Society. Niles — James Frasca.

Pennsylvania: Carlisle Barracks — Randy Hackenburg, Michael J. Winey, U.S. Army Military History Institute. Harrisburg — Debbie Frey, Historical Times. Philadelphia — Russ Pritchard, MOLLUS.

Tennessee: Chattanooga — Ida Cook, American National Bank. Clinton — Jerry Keyes. Knoxville — Elaine A. Evans, Frank H. McClung Museum. Nashville — James Kelly, Tennessee State Museum.

Virginia: Alexandria — Joan Bean, Office of the Secretary of Army. Arlington — William R. Amis. Blacksburg — Frank F. Marvin. Richmond — David C. Hahn, Museum of the Confederacy.

Washington, D.C.: Barbara Burger, Deborah Edge and staff, Still Pictures Branch, National Archives; Marylou Gjernes, U.S. Army Center of Military History; Eveline Nave, Library of Congress.

Wisconsin: Madison — Myrna Williamson, State Historical Society of Wisconsin.

The index for this book was prepared by Roy Nanovic.